David, I hope

occasion and lots

shared with Chris and Paris.

Jeannie

The Best Man's
Pocket Guide

The Best Man's Pocket Guide

Steve Bryant

GREENWICH
EDITIONS

Published in 2005 by Greenwich Editions
The Chrysalis Building
Bramley Road, London W10 6SP

An imprint of **Chrysalis** Books Group plc

This edition produced by
PRC Publishing,
The Chrysalis Building
Bramley Road, London W10 6SP

An imprint of **Chrysalis** Books Group plc

ISBN 0 86288 791 7

Printed and bound in Malaysia

Contents

Introduction

Your good friend is getting married and you have been asked to be the best man. After you have accepted and once the initial thrill of the good news has sunk in, the feeling of being honoured to be asked to play such an important role in the big day gradually wears off and the most common reaction is one of blind panic. What are my duties? How will I cope? Oh dear God I've got to stand up in front of a room full of people and make a speech! Naturally you will want to do a fantastic job for your friend, but it is quite possible that you have no idea just how to do that.

Don't panic

The whole reason for this book is that no one is ever fully prepared for being a best man when they are first asked – after all, it's not something that even the most popular person will get to do that many times in their life. Within the following pages you will find a full description of all the duties you may be expected to carry out, along with plenty of advice, hints and tips about how to do it all. There are a selection of checklists to help you to get organised and stay organised throughout the whole process. The main thing that really worries most people when they are asked to be a best man is the thought of having to write and present a speech. A large portion of this book will deal with this aspect of your duties. Advice on how to write and give a truly memorable speech is accompanied by some sample speeches and a selection of useful quotations that you may want to use. By the time you have digested all the information laid out before you, when the day of the wedding arrives you will be able to take it all in your stride and enjoy the big day.

From the outset it is worth bearing in mind that every wedding is different and that you may well not be asked or expected to fulfil all of the roles which will be discussed. It is very important that you sit down with the bride and groom and find out exactly what they do and don't require from you, both before and during the big day. Who knows, after reading this book you may well be able to offer some ideas that the groom hasn't thought of yet. After all, he probably hasn't had too much practice in the role of groom.

1
The Attributes You Will Need

❧❧❧❧

*H*istorically, a strong right arm and the ability to fight off any pursuit were the main attributes required of a best man. The tradition of asking the bride's father for his daughter's hand in marriage only dates back to around the nineteenth century. Prior to this it was not unusual for a prospective groom to kidnap the object of his affections (an act not that far removed from knocking her out and dragging her back to his cave, but a little more romantic perhaps). Anyone attempting to undertake such an endeavour alone would have been foolhardy in the extreme, so the prospective groom was accompanied by a group of fellow bachelors for support. These accomplices were known as his *groomsmen* and their role would have been to help fight off any pursuing family and friends of the bride-to-be. The tradition of the bride walking on the groom's left hand side also dates from this time as it meant that his right arm was free to wield a weapon.

By the nineteenth century the whole process had become more recognisable to the modern eye and role of the groomsmen had evolved into a far more respectable and ceremonial job. An especially close friend or relative was chosen as the best man because of his close relationship with the groom rather than for any martial prowess and the same is true today.

As the best man you, will have a variety of roles to fulfil and you will need to display a number of qualities to carry it all off successfully. If you don't know what these qualities are, or you feel that you are not naturally blessed with all the attributes you will need to make a stand-up success of your role as best man – don't worry. The most important thing is to know what you need to do and how to go about it. With the right kind of advice and preparation you will be more than capable of being a great help to the bride and groom *and* having a fantastic day yourself. By buying this book you have already demonstrated that you are taking your role seriously and you have taken a big step towards ensuring that it all goes smoothly on the day. Now let's have a closer look at the attributes that will help you.

Organisation

As the bride and groom will no doubt be able to tell you, the planning of a wedding can be a fraught business, and the whole event is actually recognised by psychiatrists as one of the three most stressful events in a person's life. One of your main functions as the best man is to take as much of the pain out of the process as possible. In order to do this you will need to be organised yourself.

Organisation may not be something that comes naturally to you: some of us are born list-makers and others have list-making thrust upon them by circumstance. In order to help those of you who are not born administrators, and as a prompt for those who are, many of the chapters within this book will end with a checklist which will summarise the main points addressed and, where appropriate, will lay out all the information you need to stay organised. It will pay to fill in the information as you go along; it would be a good idea to photocopy the relevant lists and keep a small file which you can refer to any time you need to check on something (you may want to keep the file pocket-sized so that you can keep it with you on the wedding day itself).

Obviously, you will need to get the vast majority of the information you need from the bride and groom. Once you have read this book and you have the photocopied lists, you will need to arrange to have a conversation with them. Go through their plans for the day, find out what they expect, both from the day itself and, most importantly, from you, fill in the checklists as you go along. Be sure to clarify anything which you are unsure of and don't be afraid to ask questions. The whole purpose of the meeting is to enable you to make their lives easier on the day. Note down anything which can't be answered there and then and make sure that you chase it up just as soon as possible.

You may well be pleasantly surprised at how much less daunting the whole process will seem once you have all the information set out at your fingertips. You may even enjoy being the fount of all wisdom when you are able to answer the various queries that come from guests on the day.

Sobriety

You'll want to be relaxed and have a good time, but you will also need to have a clear head to make sure that everything is running smoothly. It may well be tempting to have a few drinks to steady your nerves – just be careful. This does not mean that you can't drink at all if you want to, just be aware of your own limits.

Whilst taxis and/or nominated drivers are the norm on the stag night, you are responsible for ensuring that the groom gets home safe and sound. You can be sure that no bride will look favourably on a best man who manages to mislay the groom or return him home in a state wholly unfit for public display!

When you come to make your speech during the wedding breakfast it is a safe bet that it will not go down too well if your words are slurred or you are unable to focus on prompt cards or other props.

It's also worth bearing in mind that there is a strong possibility that there will be photographic and maybe even video evidence of your performance. If you are going to go down in recorded history you will want to be remembered for all the right reasons.

If you feel that restraint is not one of your strong points, you may want to have a word with the bar manager at the start of the day and arrange for them to stop serving you alcoholic drinks once you have reached your set limit.

Common sense

A level-headed approach should see you through any problems which may arise on the day. Whether or not you feel that common sense is one of your best attributes, it would be a good idea to make sure that you have a quiet chat with the chief bridesmaid and the bride's and groom's fathers prior to the day. Their assistance could be of great value if anything crops up which you are not sure how to handle. Remember, they all want the day to go without a hitch as much as you do, and they will be more than willing to offer any help that they can. Chances are, they will be delighted to be asked.

Your best defence against any unforeseen mishaps or events is to be as well prepared as you possibly can. For example, have a list of local taxi companies in case any of the prearranged transport breaks down, bring a portable stereo and a selection of tapes or cds in case the DJ doesn't show up for any reason. The lists within this book will cover most eventualities, but feel free to add any you may be able to think of yourself.

The wedding day will probably pass without tricky incidents, but whatever may come your way, the best thing that you can do is to remain calm and rational throughout.

Diplomacy

As the best man, part of your role is to ensure that everyone has a good time. This could mean making sure that the bride's grandmother gets to dance with a dashing young beau (yes, that's you), steering the bride and groom away from anyone who is monopolising them, or heading off any problems before they start. You will need to deal with all the people that you come into contact with during the day in a charming and polite manner.

Public speaking

The part of the day that scares most people is making *that* speech. To repeat – don't panic. There are some points to bear in mind that should help to put your mind at rest.

First, this is the most receptive audience that you will ever have: everyone is there to have a good time and they all want you to do so as well – *they are on your side.* Second, the vast majority of the guests will be reasonably merry by the time you come to make your speech and will therefore be more likely to respond well to your jokes and anecdotes.

The speech does not need be any more than five minutes long and that's no time at all, so if you are really nervous about it, bear in mind that it will be over before you know it. You need to be yourself when you make the speech – don't try to be something you are not. Most importantly, by the time you have finished reading this book you will know how to plan and present the perfect speech. Once you know how to do something it becomes a far less daunting prospect.

Patience

Everyone knows that arranging a wedding can be a stressful business, and the day itself is a nerve-wracking occasion for a number of people for all sorts of reasons. At some point tempers *will* fray, be it in the run up to the wedding or even on the day itself. You will need to be patient with all concerned and act as the peacemaker if that is necessary. Remember this day is for the bride and groom and you need to ensure that it runs as smoothly as possible. Try to be empathetic to the concerns of anyone who comes to you with a problem. If you are patient with them and remain relaxed then your attitude should rub off on them as well.

These, then, are the basics of your role, the nuts and bolts upon which you can build your performance as best man. If you can stick to these basic guidelines throughout the whole process you will be able to do a fantastic job without suffering a nervous breakdown!

2

Getting Started

One of the most basic human concerns is the fear of the unknown. At the moment you are still at the embryonic stage of your role as best man and you may be feeling that there is a vast array of knowledge which you really should have at your fingertips, but which at present you don't have a clue about. Rest assured, that's normal. As you start to gather all the information that you need and begin to get yourself and others organised, you will find the whole process becomes less daunting. Once you are aware of the whole picture and you can start to tick things off, you will find that your confidence grows as your fears recede. You will move from feeling that you are at the eye of a storm over which you have no control, to believing that you are an integral part of the planning of a great day.

Meeting the bride and groom

In order to get the ball rolling you should organise a meeting with the bride and groom. If the bride has already chosen a chief bridesmaid (and it's a fairly safe bet that if the groom has got round to asking you to be his best man the bride will have done the same with her chief bridesmaid!) it could be very helpful to have her at the meeting as well – after all, she will also be playing an important part in the proceedings.

There is no point in arranging the meeting until the bride and groom have set a date and venue for the wedding and reception (if they are to be different places). Until these details have been arranged there will not be too much for you all to discuss, and more to the point, the bride and groom will have their hands full choosing venues. Once you know that they have set a date and chosen the venue, set the wheels in motion and arrange a time and place to hold the meeting. *As soon as you have been given a definite date for the wedding it would be advisable to make sure that you put the date in your diary and cancel any other arrangements both for that day and for the day before and the day after.*

Although you are present at the wedding as the groom's main representative and helper, it is vital to bear in mind that this is the bride's big day: she is the star of the show on the day of the wedding and will almost definitely have some very strong ideas about the kind of day she wants to have. The groom obviously has an integral role to play in the planning process and on the day itself, but traditionally it is the bride who sets the overall tone for the wedding.

With luck, the bride and groom will have agreed already on most, if not all, of the details you will be discussing. However, if at any stage during the meeting there is a disagreement between the bride and groom regarding any part of the planning the golden rule for you is *don't get involved*. The best way to handle the situation would be to ask them to discuss the matter between themselves at a later date and inform you of their mutual decision. Then move on to the next part of the planning. While you may feel a natural inclination to stick up for your good friend the groom, you run the risk of alienating both him and his wife-to-be if you do get embroiled in any disagreement. This situation is unlikely to occur, but the bride and groom may be feeling tense and under a lot of pressure themselves as they go through the process of planning their wedding. They will find their own way to resolve any disputes they may have. By all means offer a sympathetic ear to the groom when the two of you are alone, as this truly is your role as a good friend and best man.

This is the point at which you will start to get a definite feel for exactly what you will be required to do in you role as best man. Use the opportunity well as it will stand you in good stead for the rest of the process. The important thing here is to be sure that you don't make assumptions: get as much solid information as you can and follow up on anything which isn't decided on the day.

Some details may change in the build-up to the wedding, but you and everyone else will be more than able to cope with these slight changes as long as you are all well-informed and well-prepared. The last thing you want is to find out at the last minute that you were expected to do something or be somewhere that you weren't aware of.

The first checklist follows at the end of this chapter and it would be a good idea to fill it in as you go along during the meeting. This will not only ensure that you don't miss anything out or forget anything, but it will also provide you with a structure for your conversation.

A lot of the information you require is composed of names and contact details for the main participants in the wedding and this won't take long to fill in. The rest may need some discussion, but you may even raise some points the bride and groom haven't considered. Before you fill in the checklist, read the following brief descriptions of some of the areas you need to cover.

Colour scheme: whether you will be wearing top hat and tails or smart suits, you will want to make sure that all the major participants look the part (in your case, the people that you are concerned with are the groom, yourself and the ushers). The bride may want you all to complement the colour scheme she has chosen for herself and her bridesmaids, or the groom may have some specific ideas of his own. Either way, you need to know if there are any definite requirements.

Suit hire: if formal suits are to be worn, in most cases they will be hired. Agree who will be in charge of organising the rental of the suits and also who will be paying for the hire. Traditionally, the bride's family will foot the bill for hired suits, but this is not always the case.

Clothing accessories: waistcoats, cufflinks, cummerbunds. All, some, or none of these may be required. You just need to know whether the bride and groom have any specific wishes about these small items.

Other considerations (clothing): every bride and groom have their own take on how they want their day to be, sartorially and in many other ways. Use this section to discuss and note down any ideas which have not been covered by the previous sections.

Car hire: if any cars or coaches are being hired for the day, agree on who is organising the hire of the vehicle/s and who is sorting out the transport on the day itself. You also need to know who is driving the various main participants between the two venues if the ceremony and reception are in different places.

Venue fees (ceremony/reception): don't worry, you won't be asked to pay for the hire of the venue! However, most venues will expect a deposit in advance and the remaining balance on the day. You may be asked to deal with settling the bill, and the groom should arrange for a cheque to be prepared ready for you to hand over to the relevant person (such as the vicar or registrar at the ceremony venue, or the events co-ordinator at the reception venue). Simply find out if you will be required to do so and contact the relevant person to arrange payment on the day. If you do settle the bill, make absolutely sure that you *get a receipt*.

Confetti: different venues have different rules regarding the use of confetti. You will need to know what types of confetti, if any, are allowed in the ceremony venue and in which areas of the venue it is permitted.

Photograph/video arrangements: if there is an official wedding video or wedding photographer, establish whether or not they will be organising their own show. You may well be asked to assist in the arrangement of different groups of people in order to help the whole process run smoothly. This is an ideal job for the ushers to help you with. Again, you may be asked to settle the bill with the photographer, and the same procedure applies as with the venue. Remember to make absolutely sure that you *get a receipt.*

Buttonholes/corsages: if it is a formal wedding and buttonholes and corsages are to be worn, agree who is arranging to provide them and who is responsible for handing them out on the day. As a rule, the best man is responsible for buttonholes for the gentlemen and the chief bridesmaid is responsible for corsages for the ladies.

Parking facilities: will the guests need to be guided to the parking facilities or to specific parking spaces? Alternatively, if coaches are being provided to transport people to the venue, will they need to be guided from the coaches to the venue? If this is the case, it also provides an ideal opportunity for the ushers to step up and lend a hand.

Order of service sheets: this is only relevant at a church wedding. Order of service sheets allow the congregation to follow the service without having to keep switching back and forth from a prayer book to a hymn book. Traditionally, the bride will arrange for the order of service sheets to be printed and the chief usher is responsible for ensuring that they are distributed. Your only role here would usually be to collect them from the bride and ensure that the chief usher passes them on to his fellow ushers.

Receiving line: will the bride and groom be having a receiving line? If they are, you need to know what part you will be playing. If there is an official toastmaster announcing the guests you may be asked to organise the guests as they enter the venue to join the receiving line, or alternatively, if there is no toastmaster, you may be asked to do the announcing. How the receiving line is managed will depend on what the bride and groom want.

Bar arrangements: the bar arrangements at receptions vary from a free bar throughout the night, to a paying bar. Establish exactly what the situation will be. Many weddings will have free drinks during the wedding breakfast and a paying bar at the reception. If there is a time or money limit on a free bar you could be asked to help ensure that all the guests receive a fair share.

Finish time: what time will the evening be ending? When will the bar be closing? Part of your role will be to ensure that the venue is cleared on time, so this is vital information (it is also the one of the questions most frequently asked of a best man).

Leaving arrangements: are the guests making their own way home/back to hotels? There may be coaches or taxis arranged to ferry people to their destinations. If so, you and the ushers will usually be asked to organise the guests at the end of the evening to make sure that everyone gets home.

Other considerations (ceremony/reception): with the wide variety of locations being used for both receptions and civil ceremonies these days, it is advisable to find out if there are any specific considerations at the venue/s. For example, some historic buildings will request that ladies do not wear stiletto heals in order to avoid damaging the floor. The vicar, registrar or event co-ordinator at any venue should have informed the bride and groom of any such stipulations, and you simply need to be aware of them and how they are to be managed.

You now have all the questions you need to discuss. Have fun with the meeting. You need to get all the information that you can, but remember that you are all there to plan a wonderful celebratory day that you will remember for the rest of your lives.

Checklist 1, First Stage Planning

Date of wedding:

Main participants:

Bride's name:

Address:

Phone:

Mobile:

E-mail:

Groom's name:

Address:

Phone:

Mobile:

E-mail:

Chief bridesmaid's name:

Address:

Phone:

Mobile:

E-mail:

Other bridesmaids' names:

Bride's parents' names:

Address:

Phone:

Mobile:

E-mail:

Groom's parents' names:

Address:

Phone:

Mobile:

E-mail:

Chief usher's name:

Address:

Phone:

Mobile:

E-mail:

Usher's name:

Address:

Phone:

Mobile:

E-mail:

Usher's name:

Address:

Phone:

Mobile:

E-mail:

Usher's name:

Address:

Phone:

Mobile:

E-mail:

Usher's name:

Address:

Phone:

Mobile:

E-mail:

Clothing:

Morning suits/smart suits:

Colour scheme:

Suit hire:

Accessories:

Other considerations:

Transport:

Car hire:

Bride to ceremony:

Groom & best man to ceremony:

Bride & groom to reception:

Bride's & groom's parents to reception:

Guests to reception:

Bride & groom to honeymoon:

Wedding venue:

Time of ceremony:

Name:

Address:

Contact name:

Contact phone no:

E-mail:

Venue fees:

Seating plan:

Confetti allowed:

Photographs/video allowed inside venue:

Photograph/video arrangements:

Buttonholes/corsages:

Order of service sheets:

Parking arrangements:

Other considerations:

Reception venue:

Time venue opens for reception:

Name:

Address:

Contact name:

Contact phone no:

E-mail:

Venue fees:

Parking arrangements:

Number of guests:

Receiving line:

Seating plan:

Meal times:

Speech times:

Bar arrangements:

Finish time:

Leaving arrangements:

Other considerations:

3
Help is at Hand

Y ou now have a great deal of the information you need at your fingertips. One of the things which has undoubtedly caught your eye while reading the previous chapter will have been the mention of delegating some tasks to the ushers. The good news here is that you have a team of helpers at your disposal. While there are certain duties which are yours and yours alone (there really is no getting out of making the speech) you can and should use the ushers to help spread the load.

Ushers

The first question that needs to be answered is how many ushers should you have? Generally speaking, the rule of thumb is that you need one usher for every twenty-five guests, so at a wedding with one hundred guests you would have four ushers including the chief usher. As with everything else, the final decision rests with the bride and groom, who may want more or less ushers for any number of reasons. The decision usually revolves around the desire to include good friends or close relatives in the proceedings. Once you know how many ushers there will be, the next question is who are they?.

Traditionally, the ushers have been brothers and close relatives of the bride and groom. However, these days they are just as likely to be other good friends of the groom. In some cases the bride and groom will have already decided on who they wish to have as their ushers; in others the groom may want to ask you for your opinion on who should be asked. If this is the case there are a number of points which you should consider when offering your advice.

While the ushers will not have such an integral role as you, the best man, they can still play a very important role on the wedding day. Like the best man, they will be the representing the groom to the rest of the guests. As such they will need to possess similar attributes to those discussed in the first chapter. As you will be asking the ushers to attend to and share some of the best man's duties, try to pick a team of helpers whom you are sure you can rely upon to take a responsible view of their roles. It is also worth bearing in mind that you should keep the chief usher up to speed with all the details and arrangements for the wedding so that if for any reason you are unable to fulfil your duties as best man he can assume the role at a moment's notice.

Other factors which you may want to consider are whether or not the ushers will have any other responsibilities on the day, such as looking after young children. Ideally, the ushers will not have far to travel to reach the wedding; it is also useful if they can all drive and have their own cars. They may be able to help with the planning of the transport or provide a back-up plan if hired cars fail to turn up for any reason.

Briefing the ushers

If the ushers are relatives of the bride and groom who you don't know well or even at all, it is a good idea to arrange a social meeting prior to the wedding. This will give you all a chance to get to know each other. After all, you are going to be expected to operate as a team at the wedding and this will be much easier to achieve if there is a relaxed and friendly atmosphere between the best man and his ushers. During this meeting you should make a point of running through the details of the wedding with the ushers to let them know what they will be asked to do. It can be helpful to provide them with a small list of their own so that there is no confusion and they are fully prepared. The other advantage of a list for the ushers is that if the meeting goes very sociably and people wake up the following day with hangovers and memory loss, they will have a written record of what is required of them.

Even if the ushers are friends that you have known for a long time it would still be a sensible idea to go for a drink and sort out the details of their duties with them. Although you will most likely meet all the ushers on the stag night, that is not the most appropriate occasion to hold a serious discussion about the organisation of the wedding.

Make sure that when you plan the night out to meet the ushers that you let everyone know that there will be a short period of the evening given over to the serious matter of wedding duties. This will avoid any possible resentment on the part of people who are expecting a good night out and are then surprised to find themselves being given a list of jobs to do at the wedding. Be equally sure that you explain to everyone that the administrative stuff will not take too long and that the rest of the night will be given over to having a good time!

The ushers' duties

The ushers should arrive at the ceremony venue roughly an hour before the service is due to start. This is because some of the guests will be travelling long distances to attend the wedding and will have left plenty of time to allow for any traffic or public transport complications.

Ensure that each of the ushers is fully aware of the duties they will need to fulfil. If the parking facilities need to be organised and/or guests need to be directed from the parking to the venue, delegate one or two of the ushers to be responsible for this. (Depending on the time of year, it is a good idea for these ushers to be armed with large golfing-style umbrellas in case of inclement weather; you really don't want a wedding full of damp and dishevelled guests.)

The chief usher and any ushers not on car park duty should be stationed at the entrance of the venue in order to greet and guide the guests as they arrive. If buttonholes and corsages are being worn, they should be distributed to the main participants on arrival. If there are any restrictions regarding the use of confetti or cameras (or any other specific requirements for your particular venue) now is a good time for the ushers to politely remind everyone of these. It is also a good idea to ask everyone to make sure that they turn off any mobile phones before the ceremony starts. It is almost traditional for at least one baby to start crying during a wedding service and there is nothing that anyone can do about this; however, the unwanted ringing of mobiles is easily avoided.

The seating plan

On arrival each guest should be met with a warm smile and a friendly greeting. This may seem like an obvious piece of advice, but as the old saying goes, "first impressions count" and this will be the guests' first impression of your friends' big day.

If hymn and prayer books or order of service sheets are not being left on individual seats in the venue they should be handed to each guest on arrival, at which point the usher should enquire whether the guests are on the bride's or groom's side.

At a formal wedding an usher will take the arm of a lady and escort her to her seat, and her husband or partner will then follow behind with any children. If two ladies arrive together the usher should escort the elder first and then return for the younger if there are not any other ushers on hand. If you are part of a formal wedding, remember this point as you may need more ushers to ensure that there is not a logjam of guests at the venue entrance waiting to be seated.

If the wedding is a less formal affair then the ushers will simply need to direct the guests to their allotted seats.

In either case the last guest to arrive will be the mother of the bride. The chief usher should escort her to her seat and then move to the back of the room to join the rest of the ushers.

The bride and groom should have informed you of their seating plan well in advance of the day for you to pass on to the ushers. As a general guide, the seating plan below is a traditional one for a church wedding.

	Groom and Best Man
Bride's parents	Groom's parents
Bride's grandparents, brothers and sisters	Groom's grandparents, brothers and sisters
Other relations of the bride	Other relations of the groom
Bride's friends	Groom's friends
Ushers	Ushers

The ushers will also need to know if there are any other considerations to bear in mind, such as access for disabled guests (where is the access and where is the easiest and best place for any disabled guests to be seated). If possible, any parents attending with very young children should be seated near the back of the venue so that if the children begin to make a noise and can't be calmed down they will not be too much of a distraction to the bride and groom and the other guests. (It also enables the parents to take them outside without too much fuss if the noise becomes overwhelming.)

If the number of guests on one side far outweighs the other and the bride and groom have not left any specific instructions, ushers should use their own judgement to even up the two sides . It is usually best to do so by redistributing friends rather than family.

One other potential area for concern regarding the seating arrangements is if either the bride's or groom's parents are divorced. Again, the bride and groom should have considered this in advance. The rule of thumb would be that if the parents are divorced and both still single they will take their traditional places. If the mother has remarried or has a new partner she will take her usual seat with her new partner and the father will be seated in the second row.

Seating at non-church ceremonies: Weddings at non-church venues have become much more commonplace in the UK since 1995 when it became legal to hold wedding ceremonies in specially licensed premises. The seating in the majority of these venues will generally be set up to mirror that in a church. There may not be permanent seating like the pews in a church, but the seats are usually arranged in two blocks on either side of a main aisle so that the bride can process down it.

The nature of the temporary seating in such establishments does, however, give the bride and groom the flexibility to do something different should they choose to do so, such as arranging the seats in a circle and holding the ceremony in the centre of the circle. If this is the case, it is vital that they provide you and the ushers with a seating plan to match their arrangements. If there is a rehearsal of the ceremony prior to the wedding, so much the better, as this will give you and the ushers the chance to accustom yourselves to the actual location.

After the ceremony: Once the ceremony is over the ushers may still have an important role to play in ensuring that the rest of the day runs smoothly. Depending on the arrangements for photographs they may be required to assist the best man in organising the guests as they are needed by the photographer. If not, they can be equally helpful in mingling with the guests to make sure that everyone is enjoying themselves and that any questions anyone might have (such as the location of the toilets) are easily answered.

After everyone has left the ceremony venue the chief usher should make a thorough check to make sure that no one has left anything behind.

At the reception: By the time you get to the reception the majority of the ushers' responsibilities are over. If the reception venue is different to the ceremony venue then the ushers may well need to do a similar parking duty to at the ceremony venue. They are also sometimes asked to help with handing out drinks to guests, and if there is to be a receiving line they will usually help the best man to get the guests organised for this. If there is a long receiving line, the ushers can also assist by ensuring that guests are not left milling around with no drink and no idea how long they will be waiting. The ushers should be aware of general information such as the timing of the meal and speeches, the location of the toilets and the bar, and venue closing times as these are questions that both they and you are most likely to be asked.

Once the guests are all seated in the reception venue ready for the wedding breakfast the ushers duties are done and they are free to enjoy the rest of the day.

The following checklist should be copied and given to all the ushers.

Checklist 2, Ushers' Duties

Best man's name:

Address:

Phone:

Mobile:

E-mail:

Chief usher's name:

Address:

Phone:

Mobile:

E-mail:

Usher's name:

Address:

Phone:

Mobile:

E-mail:

Usher's name:

Address:

Phone:

Mobile:

E-mail:

Usher's name:

Address:

Phone:

Mobile:

E-mail:

Usher's name:

Address:

Phone:

Mobile:

E-mail:

Wedding venue:

Time of ceremony:

Name:

Address:

Seating plan:

Confetti allowed:

Photographs/video allowed inside venue:

Turn off mobile phones:

Other considerations:

Duties:

Buttonholes/corsages:

Hymn/prayer books

or order of service sheets:

Escort or direct guests to seats:

Escort bride's mother to seat:

Parking duty:

Umbrella:

Assist with photographs:

Check venue for lost property:

Reception venue:

Time venue opens for reception:

Name:

Address:

Parking arrangements:

Number of guests:

Receiving line:

Meal times:

Speech times:

Bar arrangements:

Finish time:

Leaving arrangements:

Other considerations:

Duties:

Parking duty:

Receiving line:

Hand out drinks:

4
Dressing
For The Occasion

꧁ ❧ ꧂

*A*s has been said the bride will set the tone for the day. Obviously you will be expected to look smart for the big occasion. The first question to be considered is whether the bride would like the principle men (groom, best man, ushers and the bride's and groom's fathers) to wear morning suits or lounge suits. For a formal wedding the choice will most likely be morning suits; for a less formal occasion it will generally be lounge suits. In either case, the principle men will be expected to dress in a similar fashion. Remember that the same rule applies to the principle men with regard to the groom as applies to the bridesmaids and principle ladies with regard to the bride: your outfits should complement but in no way outshine his.

If you are wearing lounge suits you will be expected to foot the bill yourself, if morning suits are to be hired then traditionally the bride's family will pay. Find out in advance what the situation is, either way you will be responsible for your shoes and any accessories.

Morning suits

A traditional morning suit consists of a tailed jacket, waistcoat, trousers, top hat and gloves, usually worn with a white shirt. These days it is not unusual for people to choose to have morning suits minus the top hats and gloves, as these can be cumbersome and are generally only worn outside the venue before the ceremony and during the photographs. However, if the full morning suit is the chosen option the top hat should be removed on entering the ceremony venue and carried, along with the gloves, in the left hand thereby leaving your right hand free for shaking hands.

Morning suits come in a variety of colours, most commonly grey. If the bride has a particular colour scheme in mind for the principle men, then this should be adhered to. If the bride does not have a preference then the groom may wish to make the decision. If neither the bride or groom has a preference either way, the best bet is for all the principle man to agree to wear the same colour suits and individualise their outfit with their choice of accessory colours. Whatever option is decided upon, shoes and socks should be black, while the tie or cravat should *never* be black.

Hiring suits

Very few people will want to go the expense of buying a morning suit for a wedding If, however, you have a lifestyle which will provide ample opportunity to wear the suit on other occasions then this is not a problem. For the majority of people, weddings are the only time morning suits will be required and therefore the most sensible option is to hire the suit for the day.

The earlier you can arrange to visit a hire shop, the better, as this will ensure that they can supply your chosen suit on the day you require it; it will also allow plenty of time for any alterations which may be needed.

If suits are being hired, the bride may choose to accompany the principle men to the hire shop so that she can choose the style and colour of the outfits herself. If not, it will be up to you and the groom to organise the trip. Whether or not the bride is accompanying you, it is preferable if all the principle men can do this together. Not only will this ensure that there is a uniformity in the suits worn, it would also provide another opportunity for the principle men to get to know each other if they don't already. If this is not logistically possible then make sure that you and the groom go together with as many of the ushers as possible.

Once all the suits have been chosen a deposit will need to be paid with the balance to be settled when they are returned after the wedding. You will also need to arrange dates for the collection and return of the suits. As best man it is traditional for you to pick up the groom's suit prior to the wedding and return it after the event.

Lounge suits

It is much more common these days for the principle men at a wedding to wear lounge suits. While this may come as a relief to many men as they are not used to, and therefore not comfortable in, the more formal morning suits, it can pose a different set of problems. The advantage of morning suits is that they provide a formal and long-accepted dress code. Lounge suits encompass a huge variety of styles and colours, and it may be harder to agree on what everyone will wear. This is not a problem if the bride has a set idea of what she wants. If not it is probably easiest to agree on a colour for all the principle men to stick to.

For the same reasons as when hiring suits, if you are all going to be buying new suits for the wedding it would be best if you could all arrange to go out and buy your suits together.

Checklist 3, Wedding Suit

Hired/bought:

Who's paying:

Colour scheme:

Suit hire company:

Address:

Phone:

E-mail:

Collection date:

Return date:

Deposit:

Balance:

5
Getting There

❦

*M*aking sure that the groom gets to his wedding on time is one of the main responsibilities of the best man. While this may seem like one of the most obvious and easiest duties, you should, nonetheless, make sure that you have all the details planned well in advance and that you have back-up plans in place to cover any mishaps.

Generally, the bride's family will make all the arrangements for the transport of the bride and her party to the ceremony. It is sensible for you to be aware of the plans they have made in case of any emergency.

At a formal wedding there will probably be hired cars to transport the bride and her party to and from the ceremony venue (NB this chapter on transport is written on the assumption that the wedding venue and ceremony venue are at different locations. If they are being held in the same venue you can obviously ignore all reference to transporting people from one to the other). Generally speaking, there will be two cars for the journey to the wedding venue: one for the bride and her father, and one for the bride's mother and the bridesmaids. For the journey from the wedding to the reception there will usually be three or four cars depending on the number of bridesmaids and ushers, one for the bride and groom, one for the parents of the bride and groom and one or two for the attendants.

Every groom's worst nightmare is that bride doesn't turn up on the big day. He will be nervous enough as it is, so if there is any delay in the bride's arrival it will only increase his fretfulness. With luck, the bride's party will also have taken all possible precautions to ensure that there are no problems getting to the venue on time, but if there is a delay for any reason you should be kept informed of the reasons and an estimated time of arrival. The groom will feel much better if he knows that the bride is merely delayed!

The bride's father is your best bet as the point of contact should there be any delay as he will be in the bridal car and it's not something the bride will want to be concerned with on her wedding day, as she has enough to worry about already! Speak to the bride's father well in advance and ensure that you have his mobile phone number and that he has both yours and that of the chief usher.

There are two ways you can play this should the bride's father need to contact you: either have your phone in your trouser pocket on vibrate only (do *not* have it set to ring as you and the groom will be waiting inside the venue in front of all the guests), and ask that he rings you or else that he calls the chief usher (who will be waiting outside the venue to escort the bride's mother when she arrives) who can then discreetly come and inform you and the groom of any hold-up.

If there is a delay you should inform the vicar or registrar straight away. You do not need to make any announcement to the guests unless it is going to be a long delay.

It is also worth consulting the bride and groom to find out if there will be any guests coming by public transport who will need to be collected from the station and ferried to the venue. Whilst this is not strictly one of your duties as best man, in the general spirit of lightening the load on the bride and groom, it is an area in which you and the ushers can be a real help. If this is the case you will not want to tie up yourself or the ushers for too long as you all have other duties and guests that you will need to attend to. If possible, contact the people concerned and arrange for them to arrive around an hour-and-a-half before the ceremony starts, or else try to find out if there are any other guests who live locally or who are staying in local hotels the night before the wedding who could help out with collecting people from the station.

Using a hired car: If you are using a hired car to transport yourself and the groom to the wedding, make sure that you book it well in advance and that you confirm the booking a couple of days before the wedding. You will also need to make sure that you have the following information. Is the car being delivered or do you need to collect it? Note the date and time for delivery or collection, and the date and time that the car needs to be returned. Check that the car will be clean and have a full tank of petrol. Be sure that you confirm all the hire charges and when they need to be paid. *Never* pay fully in advance as this leaves you with no leverage if there is a problem on the day.

One consideration you should bear in mind is letting some of the practical jokers who are attending the wedding *know* that it is a hired car and not to be tampered with. At one wedding I attended, some wag borrowed a lipstick to daub suitable messages on the side of the departing car. The lipstick soon ran out leaving a metal rim which was then gouged into the paintwork of the car. Not the best of starts to a new life together!

Using your own car: It is far more common for the groom and best man to travel in their own transport, after all you will be arriving at the venue before the majority of the guests so there is no need to create a big impression. If this is the case you should make sure that you have your car serviced thoroughly a couple of weeks before the wedding day to ensure that there is as little chance as possible of a breakdown *en route*. Either clean the car yourself, or even better, get it valeted a couple of days before the wedding. Give it one last check the night before, make sure that you have a full tank of petrol and add any decoration (such as ribbons) that you intend to use. If possible park your car in a garage as this means that if there is a downpour overnight your decorations will not be ruined and the car will not be dirty.

Plan the journey: Wherever you and the groom are staying the night before the wedding you should make sure that you have planned out your route from there to the ceremony venue well in advance. Even if it is a local route that you are familiar with, you should test-drive it a couple of times so that you have a good idea of the journey time (if you or the ushers are helping to collect people from the station on the day it is also a good idea to do the same for the route from the station to the venue). Try to undertake your test-drives on the same day and at the same time as the wedding is being held as this will give you a better indication of an accurate time scale. You should also find out if there will be any other factors such as road works or a village fete on the day itself as these could have an impact on your journey time.

You should aim to arrive at the church at least thirty minutes before the ceremony is due to start, which will leave some spare time should anything untoward happen. You may want to aim to arrive at the same time as the ushers as this will give you a last chance to brief them and ensure that they all know what is expected of them. The wishes of the groom should also be taken into consideration, though, as he may not want to be hanging around outside the venue for that long.

The ushers should follow the same process as you in terms of planning out a route and test-driving it to ensure that they have a realistic idea of how long it will take them to get to the venue.

Travelling to the reception: Again, you will need to check with the bride and groom about the arrangements they have made. They may have booked coaches to convey all the guests to the reception, or simply asked guests to make their way in their own cars.

If coaches or any other form of transport is being provided to convey the guests to the reception, the ushers should be asked to help organise the guests onto the transport. You and the chief usher should travel in one of the first coaches or in your own car so that you can direct the guests when they get to the reception venue.

If the guests are asked to provide their own transport there could well be some who will be left high and dry. Sit down with the bride and groom a few weeks before the wedding and work out who on the guest list will not have their own transport. The easiest way to remedy this is to ask around the other guests to find out who has spare room in their cars to help. Chances are that most of the people who will need a lift to the reception will be the same ones who needed to be collected from the station. The plans and people you had in place to collect them from the railway station can probably be replicated with a few minor adjustments to take them to the reception. Again, you will need to make sure that you are one of the first to arrive at the reception venue so that you can direct guests if needed.

The end of the night: Traditionally, the bride and groom leave the reception half an hour before their guests to set off for their honeymoon. Generally speaking, the groom will drive the happy couple off to their chosen location or they will have hired either a taxi or or a chauffeured car to transport them. If there is a hired car or a taxi involved it is worth booking early and confirming the booking a couple of days beforehand; check with the groom as to whether or not he is organising this or whether he would like you to do so. (He will probably have organised the transport but might appreciate you confirming the bookings in the run-up to the wedding).

If the groom is driving then you have the chance to indulge in one of the more pleasurable traditions for the best man. Oh yes, it's time to redecorate the groom's car. He's put you through all the stress and headache of helping him to organise and run his wedding and while you have been more than happy to do so and have probably had a great time doing it, the chance to have some small measure of recompense is not to be sniffed at. Balloons, shaving foam and empty tin cans tied to the back of the car are the most common items used, but you can let your imagination run riot. One word of caution: make sure that nothing is done that will in any way damage the car permanently or that will endanger the bride and groom as they drive off. It would be a thoughtful gesture if you were to provide some basic cleaning equipment for the groom to enable him to clean up his car (some cloths, a *firmly* sealed bottle of water, a penknife for any string and some wet wipes for the bride and groom to clean themselves up should do the job).

Emergency planning

This section on transport has referred to a number of things which might suggest that you will spend all day chasing around sorting out breakdowns and other problems. Remember that, as with much of the advice within this book, these are all worst-case scenarios, and you would be extremely unlucky to have even a few of them happen to you on the day of your friends' wedding. The aim is for you to be prepared for all possible eventualities, *not* frighten the life out of you.

With this in mind, there are a couple of other things which you might like to consider. Make sure that all the principle men (you, the groom, at least the chief usher if not all the ushers and the father of the bride) have mobile phones and that you all have each other's numbers. This will enable you to stay in contact if there are any problems. If anyone doesn't have a mobile phone it would be advisable to buy or borrow one; and if anyone does buy a new phone or borrow one they will need to make sure that they are familiar with how to use it by the day of the wedding. It is also a good idea to have the phone numbers of a few local taxi firms, just in case. You would be well advised to ring the taxi firms a few days beforehand to get a rough idea of how long it would take to get a taxi on the day and time of the wedding. Make sure that you have plenty of cash on you, as well as credit cards.

Checklist 4, Transport

Car hire:

Company name:

Phone number:

Collection/delivery date/time:

Deposit:

Return date/time:

Balance due:

Own car:

Service date booked:

Clean car:

Decoration:

Journeys:

Time to ceremony venue:

Check if any other events on wedding date:

Taxi company:

Phone number:

Estimated time to order:

Taxi company:

Phone number:

Estimated time to order:

Taxi company:

Phone number:

Estimated time to order:

Guests to collect from station:

(Include time and station name/location)

Who is collecting them:

Method of transport to reception:

Guests who need a lift to reception:

Who is giving them a lift:

Mobile phone numbers:

Groom:

Bride's father:

Chief usher:

Usher:

Usher:

Usher:

6
The Stag Night

*O*rganising and participating in the stag night is, generally speaking, the job that best men look forward to the most. This is the groom's last big night out as an unmarried man and, as such, is usually quite a riotous affair. It is also the one area connected with weddings where tradition is adhered to less and less frequently. In the past, the stag night was held the night before the wedding, although why anyone ever considered this to be a good idea is beyond belief, bearing in mind the nature of the event. There are numerous stories, not all of them apocryphal, of grooms waking up in the wrong town on the day of their own wedding.

Unless you and your friends are all teetotallers, under no circumstances should you and the groom plan to hold the stag night the night before his wedding! It is a safe bet that just about everyone who attends the stag night will wake up the next day feeling at least a little the worse for wear, and this is no way to prepare for a wedding. Think about all the duties you, as best man, have to attend to and imagine trying to perform them with a ringing head, feeling like you've just gone ten rounds with Mike Tyson. More to the point, think about you and the groom having to face his bride-to-be the following day in such a state – neither of you will win any popularity polls. Ideally, the stag night should be arranged for *at least* a week before the wedding to give all concerned plenty of time to recuperate. Depending on the kind of event you are planning, it is not unusual these days for the stag night to be up to a month or more in advance of the wedding.

Who should be invited?

Traditionally, this is a night for unmarried men only, but it is much more common for the groom to invite those whom he considers close friends and relatives regardless of their marital status. Sit down with the groom and get a list from him of all those who he would like to invite to his stag night. This should be done as far in advance of the agreed date as possible to allow people plenty of time to make arrangements to attend. Brothers of the bride and the bride's and groom's fathers are traditionally invited (with the fathers leaving early), but it is really just a matter of personal choice for the groom. It is unusual for formal invitations to be issued for a stag night, and generally the event is organised over the phone or via e-mail. Once you and the groom have agreed a date and he has given you a list of those he would like to invite, you should contact everyone straight away to confirm the eventual number who can attend.

Where to go and what to do

The term 'stag night' can be a bit of a misnomer as the event can range from a drink in the the local pub to a trip abroad for the weekend, with just about anything imaginable in-between; activities such as paint-balling, golfing days and go-carting are increasingly popular. The two overriding considerations here should be what the groom wants to do (if the wedding is the chiefly the bride's big day, this is most certainly the groom's big night out), and the financial positions of all those whom he wishes to attend. There is no point in planning an expensive weekend away with all sorts of fun activities if half the of people who will be invited can't afford to come (or worse will feel obliged to come and put themselves in debt to do so). If you or the groom have a rough idea of the financial positions of all the people who he wants to invite, you should plan accordingly; if not it may require some careful investigation from you when you make the initial phone calls to invite people.

There is such a huge variety of possibilities for stag night celebrations that it could take a whole book just to list them. The groom will have some kind of idea as to what he would like to do and you may well have some suggestions of your own. If you are struggling for inspiration beyond the traditional night out at a pub or club, there are numerous web sites dedicated to planning a stag do. Just put "stag night" into any internet search engine and you will be presented with a plethora of options offering just about any kind of day/night/weekend you can think of. If you do organise a group booking at a restaurant/club or similar venue, let them know when you make the booking that it is a stag party that will be attending as some venues will not look favourably on a large male group arriving unannounced. The last thing you want is to organise the perfect stag night, only to be turned away at the door.

Who foots the bill?

Traditionally, the groom foots the bill for the entire stag night, but as you can see from just some of the ideas already mentioned, this is unlikely to be feasible (although you might enjoy letting the groom know of this tradition if he starts to let his imagination run away with him when you are planning the night out). It is quite common for all the participants at a stag do to pay their own way (hence the importance of making sure that they can all afford whatever is planned) or for the groom to put some money in the pot to start with and once this has run out people then pay for themselves.

If everyone is paying their own way ensure that everyone is fairly treated by organising a whip, or kitty at the start of the evening. As best man you would be expected to organise this and attend to the buying of drinks and settling of bills from the whip. The best bet is to agree how much each person should put into the whip beforehand, and to make sure that everyone knows both how much it is and how it will work. This will avoid any potential arguments on the night itself (because, let's be honest, a large party of drunk men is not always the most rational group of people).

Speech!

Another tradition that is not always followed, quite possibly to your relief, is for the best man to make a speech on the stag night. This one should really be a matter of personal choice for the best man unless the groom is particularly keen for you to do so. If this is the case, though, the groom should also be aware that he will be expected to make a speech himself in response to yours. The ideal time for these speeches is at the end of a meal, although depending on the kind of night you have planned there may not be an appropriate time for them (if you are in a pub for the night followed by a club, for example there probably won't be an opportunity).

If you really do not like the idea of giving a speech at the wedding it is worth bearing in mind that the stag night could be an ideal time for a rehearsal, which might help to boost your confidence for the big day. (But if you really don't want to and feel it will spoil your enjoyment of the evening, you don't have to.) You will be probably be with a group of friends with whom you feel comfortable and while you can probably expect to be heckled to some extent, it will be done in a good-natured way. It also provides you with a chance to tell all those jokes and stories about the groom that you won't be able to tell at the wedding (although if the bride's and groom's fathers are present you should temper your choices with this in mind).

For hints on how to prepare and present your speech, refer to the later section in this book on the best man's speech at the wedding (possibly taking a little less notice of the advice regarding not drinking). The generally expected contents for the best man's speech at a stag do are as follows:

* Funny stories from the groom's childhood and or university days (you can embarrass him, just not *too* much. Now is not the time to reveal any secrets you have been entrusted with over the years).
* All the poor unfortunate girls who have been passed over by the groom or who will never have the pleasure of his "company".
* How he might attempt to "train" his future wife to his way of living.
* How in reality his bachelor days are over and he is in fact soon to be retrained by his bride to be (this should be done with care. Under no circumstances should you insult his bride).
* Offer advice on how he might attempt to avoid his fate if he gets cold feet (provide the phone numbers of various embassies for emigration advice, or suggest he joins the French Foreign Legion, for example).

Transport

Depending on the kind of event you have planned, the method of transport could be anything from walking to the pub, to catching flights to and from your destination. One thing which definitely won't change is your responsibility to make absolutely sure that the groom gets home safe and sound at the end of the night/weekend. Leaving him naked and tied to a lamppost may seem like a good idea at the time, but in the cold light of day (not to mention faced with the cold fury of his bride-to-be), you will undoubtedly regret it.

The essential thing is to make sure that whatever you are doing, you have the transport planned well in advance and that everyone who is attending knows the details. It is highly unlikely that you will have nominated drivers at a stag do (after all what's the point of attending if you can't join in all the fun), but if you do have a few drivers ensure that they don't drink. If not, make sure that no one drives under any circumstances. As on the day of the wedding, make sure that you have the phone numbers of a few local taxi companies and some cash in reserve should it be needed.

Checklist 5, Stag Night

Attendees:

Name:

Phone number:

E-mail:

Name:

Phone number:

E-mail:

Name:

Phone number:

E-mail:

Name:

Phone number:

E-mail:

Name:

Phone number:

E-mail:

Name:

Phone number:

E-mail:

Name:

Phone number:

E-mail:

Name:

Phone number:

E-mail:

Name:

Phone number:

E-mail:

Name:

Phone number:

E-mail:

Name:

Phone number:

E-mail:

Name:

Phone number:

E-mail:

Name:

Phone number:

E-mail:

Name:

Phone number:

E-mail:

Name:

Phone number:

E-mail:

Name:

Phone number:

E-mail:

Name:

Phone number:

E-mail:

Name:

Phone number:

E-mail:

Name:

Phone number:

E-mail:

Name:

Phone number:

E-mail:

Name:

Phone number:

E-mail:

Name:

Phone number:

E-mail:

Location:

Name:

Contact name:

Phone number:

Other details:

Budget per person:

Transport:

Airport:

Flight company:

Flight time:

Check in time:

Terminal:

Return airport:

Return flight time:

Return check in time:

Return terminal:

Hired car/taxi company:

Phone number:

Pick up location:

Pick up time:

Collection location:

Collection time:

Deposit:

Balance due:

Local taxi firms:

Name:

Phone number:

Name:

Phone number:

Name:

Phone number:

7
The Lead-up To The Wedding

❧❧❧

Wedding rehearsal

Depending on the venue at which the wedding is being held, there may be a rehearsal during the week leading up to the day of the wedding. This can provide an ideal opportunity not only for the bride and groom to run through the ceremony, but also for the rest of the main participants to familiarise themselves with each other, the venue and their specific roles during the ceremony.

The best man should definitely be present for any rehearsal and, ideally, all the ushers (if this is not possible you should try to arrange for the chief usher to be present at the very least),. This is particularly relevant if there are any parking arrangements that the ushers need to be learn about, or if the bride and groom have chosen an unconventional seating plan. It will be particularly helpful if both you and the ushers have names and faces to put to the families of the bride and groom if you don't already know them, as this will stand you in good stead when the guests are greeted as they arrive and later when you are helping to organise the photographs. If there are any remaining details regarding the wedding which need to be clarified, now is the time to do so.

After the rehearsal the bride and groom may choose to host some form of small party or meal for the main participants to thank them for all their help in getting the wedding organised. If this is the case, it is the perfect time for you to present your wedding gift to the bride and groom. The bride and groom can use the opportunity to give out any gifts that they wish to present to the best man, ushers and bridesmaids.

The day before the wedding

If at all possible, the best man should try to ensure that he has the day before the wedding free. As you will have already gathered, the preparations for a wedding can be a hectic business and while the day before is not the time to be making any new plans or arrangements, it is the ideal time to tie up all the loose ends and to make sure that as much as possible is in place to guarantee that the wedding day will run as smoothly as possible. If you are unable to make yourself free on the day prior to the wedding it would be advisable to try to make sure that you have organised all the items mentioned during the week leading up to the wedding.

One of your main functions will be to help the groom with any last-minute nerves he has about the big day ahead and to act as a go-between for the bride. There are bound to be a few phone calls from the bride to check that the groom hasn't forgotten to do something that he should, or even just to make sure that he is feeling ok and that everything is on schedule. These are the classic symptoms of pre-wedding nerves on all sides and your role is to assuage the worries of all concerned.

In order to be able to honestly keep everyone else calm, and for your own peace of mind, you will need to make sure that you are on top of all the areas that you are directly responsible for. To this end there are a few things that you should check on the day before the wedding:

* Has the groom got the wedding rings and are they in a safe place?
* Has the groom got the certificate of banns or the marriage licence?
* Make sure that you have collected any hired clothing and checked that it is all clean and fits properly.
* Check that any clothing which isn't hired is cleaned, pressed and ready to wear. Check that the same is true for the groom.
* Check that you have any and all accessories (i.e. cufflinks) that you will be wearing laid out and ready to wear. Check that the same is true for the groom.
* Phone the chief usher to make sure that he is likewise prepared and that he knows exactly what he needs to do the following day. Ask him to phone his team of ushers and ensure that they, too ,are fully prepared.
* Confirm any bookings for hired cars or taxis.
* Check that all the transport arrangements for guests are in place and everything is covered.
* If buttonholes and corsages are being worn, check with the florist that they have the order.
* If the bride and groom are going on honeymoon directly from the reception or from their hotel the

following day, make sure that the groom has all the relevant documents, his passport, any foreign currency and his credit cards all packed and ready to go. Make sure that he has packed for his honeymoon, as he won't have time on his wedding day!

* If order of service sheets are being used, pick them up from the printers or the bride's mother (if you are really busy and he is free you may want to ask the chief usher to do this as it is he and the ushers who will need them).

* Has the groom got the wedding rings and are they in a safe place? (You can never be too careful. . .)

All of the above could take all day to get through or it could be the work of a couple of hours – it will all depend to a large degree on how well-organised other people (notably the groom) are. If it does all go without a hitch it would be a nice gesture to phone the bride and ask if there is anything outside your traditional remit that you could help out with. There may be a few errands that still need to be run and you could be an invaluable help if people are stretched to get everything done. Remember, though that you should only do so once you are fully satisfied that you have everything your end completely under control and that the groom does not need you for anything himself as he is your primary concern.

The morning of the wedding

Whatever time of day the wedding is being held, you are going to be busy on the morning itself and you will need to be up and about with plenty of time to spare. You will also need be at your most efficient on this, of all, days. If you are not naturally an organised person you may want to use the timetable planner at the end of this section to help you get to grips with how long it will take you to get through all of your tasks and still stay sane enough to act as a source of support for the groom.

The first thing you will need to do once you have decided what time you to get up is to take whatever action is necessary to make sure that this does happen – you *cannot* afford to be late. Set more than one alarm, arrange an alarm call on your mobile, and in the extreme, if you really are very bad at getting up in the morning, arrange for someone more reliable to come round and physically drag you out of bed. (If you do feel you need to do this, ensure that whoever you have asked has a key to let themselves in, otherwise they could be left hanging on the doorbell while you sleep the morning away.) Once you are out of bed yourself, you should call the groom and make sure that he, too, is up and about. If he is a terrible riser then you may need to take on the task of going round to get him out of bed (again, a spare key would be vital). If you do have to physically get the groom out of bed it is probably best to take all your clothes and any other items you need for the day with you and plan to start your day from his house.

It might be a good idea to arrange to stay with the groom on the night before the wedding, as this means that you will have double the chance of ensuring that you are both up on time. It will also provide the groom with a good friend to talk to on his last night as a bachelor, and this could be ideal if he is suffering from any pre-wedding nerves.

After you have assured yourself that you and the groom are both up and getting underway, you should phone the chief usher and make sure that he too is out of bed and that he has phoned the other ushers to make sure that they are also getting ready. Have one last brief run through with the chief usher so that you are both confident that everyone knows what needs to be done and when it needs doing.

If you are using any hired transport on the day, ring the company and confirm the bookings. Even if you have done so the previous day this is still a wise precaution if for no other reason than to put your own mind at rest (it is also quite possible that you will speak to a different person than on the previous day and it will do no harm to have confirmed the booking with the person working on the actual day of hire).

You should definitely make sure that both you and the groom have a decent breakfast on the morning of the wedding. You will be expending a lot of nervous, if not physical, energy during the day and, depending on the time of the ceremony, you might not have the chance to eat again until the reception. It is entirely possible that neither of you will feel hungry on the morning of the wedding because of nerves, but you should still make sure that you do have something substantial to eat. If the groom is going to be using his own car to transport himself and his bride away from the reception and you are responsible for ensuring that it gets there before the wedding, you should check that the car is clean, has a full tank of petrol and is running well.

You should also make sure before you leave that the groom has packed all the suitcases he will need (paying particular and stringent attention to any relevant documentation) if he and the bride are going directly on their honeymoon from the reception. Make sure that you have allowed yourself plenty of time to deliver the car to the reception venue and return to the groom's house.

Depending on the time of the wedding and how well things are running for you and the groom, you may find that you have some spare time on your hands. If this is the case you could phone the bride or her father to find out if there are any last-minute errands that they need help with. As with the previous day though, you should not commit to doing anything that will jeopardise your own timetable. If you do not have the time to spare to offer your services to help, ring anyway just to let everyone there know that all is running smoothly with you and the groom and to wish them all good luck for the big day ahead.

It would be advisable to wait to get changed into your wedding outfit until after you have eaten and completed all your other tasks, as the last thing you want is to turn up at the wedding with a stained or torn suit or tie. Before you leave, do one final check that you have all the things you will need.

* Take the rings from the groom and put them in a safe
  pocket that you will be able to access easily.
* Take a spare set of rings (any cheap, plain substitute
  will do – this really is just a last-ditch back-up in case
  of emergency).
* Fully charged mobile phone with all appropriate
  phone numbers.
* Your speech or prompt cards.
* Credit cards and plenty of cash.
* A big umbrella or two just in case of inclement
  weather.
* Any items to decorate the groom's car if you are
  going to do so (don't forget to pack a clean-up kit as
  well though!).

Once all your tasks are completed and you are suited and booted, it's time to
collect the groom and head off to the wedding venue.

Wedding Morning Timetable Planner

Time: *Task:*

....   **Wake-up**

....   **Wash and dress in casual clothes**

....   **Phone groom**

....   **Phone chief usher**

....   **Confirm any transport bookings**

....   **Go to groom's house (if not already there)**

....   **Have breakfast**

.... **Check all clothes and accessories**

.... **Groom's car to reception**

.... **Check own car (decorate if appropriate)**

.... **Phone bride/bride's father**

.... **Get dressed for wedding**

.... **Check you have all the things you need**

.... **Leave for ceremony**

8
The Wedding
Ceremony

T he exact nature of the ceremony will depend largely on the venue at which the wedding is going to take place. In this chapter we will look at a wide variety of the services you may come across, starting with the traditional Church of England ceremony. This will be described in detail as a basic guide to the wedding ritual, and following that we shall examine the variations in other services, both religious and secular. These will include Roman Catholic, Jewish and non-conformist weddings (Presbyterian and Methodist), along with the procedures you will come across at a civil wedding at a registry office, or at an alternative venue, such as the centre circle of a famous local football club.

Church of England ceremony

Make sure you and the groom arrive at the church in plenty of time for the ceremony. If you need to have a final chat with the ushers, aim to get there about thirty minutes before the start. Whatever your plans, you should arrive no later than fifteen minutes before the start time, which will allow the groom to be settled inside the church and enable you to have a quick check with the ushers that everything is running smoothly. The groom will probably be jumping like a cat on a hot tin roof and in need of a bit of moral support. On arrival at the church you may need to steer the groom diplomatically away from various well-wishers – he only has a small amount of time to stop and say hello to guests, and you should both be inside the church and seated in the front row on the right with no less than ten minutes to go. You certainly do not want the bride to turn up while the groom and guests are still outside, as this will ruin her big entrance.

Depending on the arrangements that have been made with the minister this may be the time to present him with the groom's banns certificate and settle the church fees. If not, it will probably be done just after the register has been signed.

The last two cars to arrive should be those containing the bride's mother and the bridesmaids, followed by the bride and her father. The bridesmaids will wait in the porch for the bride while the chief usher escorts the bride's mother to her seat in the front row on the left hand side. The chief usher should then make his way to the back of the church and take his seat. All the other ushers bar one should also take their seats at the back of the church. The remaining usher should wait outside until the bride is ready to make her entrance, at which point he will signal to the organist who will begin to play the bride's chosen processional music. Once the bride, her father and the bridesmaids have all entered the church and begun to walk down the aisle the last usher should quietly shut the church doors and take his seat.

As the processional music starts up the congregation will rise to their feet. You and the groom should also rise at this point and turn sideways to greet the bride as she makes her way down the aisle. The groom will no doubt be eager to get his first look at his beautiful bride on their wedding day. When the bride is roughly half-way down the aisle the best man and the groom should turn to face the front of the church and take their positions for the ceremony, the groom slightly to the right of centre facing the minister, and the best man a step behind and to the right of him.

The bridal procession stops when the bride draws level with the groom on his left, and the father of the bride releases his daughter's arm and takes a step back and to the left of her. The chief bridesmaid will come forward and lift the bride's veil if she is wearing one, take her bouquet and make any necessary adjustments to her train. The chief bridesmaid then takes her place just behind the bride. In the event that there are no bridesmaids, the bride can hand her bouquet to her father who will pass it on to her mother to look after during the ceremony.

The precise running order and contents of the service may vary slightly, but will generally follow the pattern below:

> Bride's entrance (processional music)
> Hymn, reading or prayer
> The marriage ceremony
> Prayers
> Address from the minister
> Hymn
> Blessing
> Signing of the register
> Bride and groom exit followed by the congregation
> (recessional music)

Throughout the hymn, reading or prayer and the beginning of the marriage ceremony, the best man and the bride's father maintain their positions slightly behind the bride and groom. The minister will begin by explaining the reason for the gathering in the church and the religious significance of marriage. He will next inquire if anyone present knows of a valid reason why the couple cannot be married, and, assuming there is no answer, he will ask the same question of the bride and groom. The bride and groom are asked in turn to take each other as husband and wife. Once they have both answered in the affirmative, the minister will ask who is giving the bride away. At this point the bride's father (or whoever is representing him) should pass the bride's right hand to the minister. Traditionally the bride's father does so in silence, but many fathers will say "I do" at this point. The bride and groom then exchange their vows and when they are complete the minister will present the open prayer book to the best man so that he can place the wedding rings on it. The best man and the bride's father should then return to their seats for the remainder of the service.

Once the service has been completed, the minister will lead the wedding party to sign the register. This will either be in the vestry or at a table set aside within the main body of the church. The exact location will depend upon the church in which the marriage is being held, and if there has been a wedding rehearsal, you will all know where you are going; if not, simply follow the minister's lead. The order in which the wedding party proceeds to the signing of the register is:

> Bride and groom
> Chief bridesmaid and best man
> Bridesmaids
> Bride's mother and groom's father
> Groom's mother and bride's father

Before you begin the walk to sign the register, have a quick check to make sure that the chief bridesmaid has remembered the bride's bouquet; if not you should pick it up and take it through. Also, if you are wearing full formal suits be sure to take both your hat and gloves, and those of the groom as you will need these for the recessional (the processional exit from the church). All the gentlemen paired with ladies should stand on the right hand side and offer the lady their left arm to escort her.

The bride and groom sign the register followed by two witnesses – these usually be will be either the best man and the chief bridesmaid, or the bride's and groom's fathers. This is a decision which the bride and groom will have made prior to the wedding and you should all know in advance who will be doing so.

If you did not settle the church fees with the minister on arrival at the church you should wait behind for a brief moment and do so now.

The order of procession as the wedding party leaves the signing of the register and leads the congregation out of the church is the same as that going to the signing. The usher who earlier closed the church doors should open them as the party begins to move up the aisle.

Once the congregation has left the church it is time for the official photographs to be taken. Theoretically, this should take around twenty to thirty minutes, but depending on the number of guests at the wedding and how organised everyone is, it can take an awful lot longer. This is where you can be of great help to the bride and groom and the photographer. The guests will quite naturally be engaged in conversation, catching up with old friends and relatives that they haven't seen for a long time. You should make yourself available to the photographer between each picture to gather the appropriate people quickly and politely for each shot. As you will be in a lot of the pictures yourself and because there will be a number of disparate groups which will need to be bought together, this is definitely a job where the ushers can be enormously helpful.

If you have the misfortune to be attending a wedding on a day when the weather is inclement and unsuitable for photographs, it would be a good idea to suggest that the photographer takes a few pictures of the bride and groom in the church porch (possibly with one or two attendants such as the bride's mother and father, and the groom's mother and father) and then take the rest of the photographs indoors at the reception. If, however, the bride and groom have their hearts set on having their photographs taken at the church you should accede to their wishes and help to organise them as quickly and efficiently as possible.

When the photographs have all been taken, it's time to move on to the reception venue. You should escort the bride and groom to their car as they will be the first to leave, no doubt waved off by the rest of the guests. At a formal wedding the bride and groom will be followed by the bridesmaids, the bride's parents and then the groom's parents. Once all the main participants have been sent on their way the rest of the guests will follow.

Traditionally, the best man will wait to ensure that all the guests have left for the reception before he makes his own way there. However, you may be more useful at the reception venue, in which case assign the chief usher to ensure that everyone else is looked after. (All the transport arrangements should have been well planned in advance so that he will know who is going with who.) Make sure that before he leaves he has a final check to collect any items that have been forgotten or left behind in the church and grounds by any of the guests.

Double weddings

Conducting two weddings at the same time is a very rare occurrence but it does happen, usually if the two brides are sisters or if the two grooms are brothers who wish to share their nuptials. If this is the case, the two couples should get together beforehand to arrange the details of how the ceremony and order of precedence will work. As best man you will fulfil all the same functions for your groom as if the wedding were a single marriage, although it would be a good idea to make sure that you have had a chance to run through the plans for the day with the other best man to ensure that you both know exactly who will be doing what when. The traditional arrangements for such an event are as follows.

If the brides are sisters, then the elder takes precedence and her party is considered the senior. When walking down the aisle the senior bride will be on her fathers right arm and the junior on his left, with each followed by their chief bridesmaid and retinue.

If the grooms are brothers, then again, it is the eldest who takes precedence and is considered the senior. In this case the bride of the senior groom will walk down the aisle followed by her retinue who will in turn be followed by the junior bride and her retinue.

How and where all the participants will stand during the service will depend upon the space available in the church where the wedding is being held. In this case a full rehearsal is essential as the potential for people to get confused on the day is far greater than at a single wedding. The same is also true of the seating in the church: the two couples must ensure that the best men, and in turn the ushers, know exactly where all the guests are to be seated.

The senior couple will take their vows first, followed by the junior couple. When the couples move to sign the register, it is the senior couple and their retinue who go first, followed by the junior couple. The register is signed in the same order.

For the recession, the two parties should be complete units, so the full retinue of the senior couple make their way from the signing of the register back up the aisle, followed by the full party of the junior couple.

There is no reason why the two best men should not join forces and act as a team when it comes to organising the photographs and ensuring that all the guests get to the reception. Once there, if there is a receiving line, there is usually only one.

When it comes to the speeches at the reception, it is traditional for only one best man to speak, simply so that the speeches do not go on for too long. In this case it is generally accepted that the best man of the senior couple will make the speech. However, if he feels that the other best man would do a better job, the junior best man can do it. A growing number of grooms employ two best men and it is not that unusual for joint speeches to be made. There is no reason why you shouldn't do this as long as both of the best men are comfortable doing so.

Roman Catholic weddings

For a Roman Catholic wedding to be legally recognised in England, the bride and groom will need to obtain a licence from the superintendent registrar prior to the wedding. The majority of Roman Catholic priests are authorised to register marriages, but it is important to check this well in advance. If the priest is not authorised the couple will have to arrange for a registrar to be present when the register is signed.

For a full Nuptial Mass (Marriage celebrated during Mass) to be carried out, both the bride and groom must be Catholic; if one or other are not, then a more simple ceremony (Marriage outside of Mass) is performed. It is possible for a non-Catholic and a Catholic to have a full Nuptial Mass but this requires the permission of the Catholic partner's parish priest.

The order of service and the content in a Catholic wedding follow a similar pattern to that in the Church of England, so the duties of the best man are likewise very similar. The best man and the father of the bride position themselves in the same places in the church and the best man fulfils the duty of holding the rings and presenting them to the priest after the exchange of rings (the priest will proffer a silver dish rather than an open prayer book for the best man to place the rings on). It is also traditional for the groom to present his bride with gold and silver.

Once the marriage has been blessed the bride and groom, along with their two chosen witnesses, (generally the best man and the chief bridesmaid) follow the priest to the sacristy where the civil declaration is made and the register signed.

At a Marriage outside of Mass this is the end of the service and the bride and groom and their attendants proceed out of the church as with a Church of England service to have their photographs taken.

If a full Nuptial Mass is being held, then the bridal party returns to the church, the best man, chief bridesmaid and other attendants return to their seats in the front rows, and the bride and groom take their place behind the sanctuary rails. It is also now that any member of the congregation who wishes to take Holy Communion will have the opportunity to do so. Once the Mass has concluded the bride and groom lead the recession out of the church.

Jewish weddings

Couples who wish to be married under Jewish rites must be able to provide proof that they are both Jewish. Documentation which shows that both sets of parents were married under Jewish rites is usually sufficient.

It is very rare for the best man at a Jewish wedding not to be of the Jewish faith. As much as anything, this is because the best man is traditionally a brother of the groom (*chatan*); if he has no brothers the best man is selected from the bride's brothers (*kallah*); if neither bride nor groom have any brothers, it is traditional to ask a male relative. If you are a non-Jew asked to be the best man at a Jewish friend's wedding you will need to get the precise details of the service from the groom because, as with other faiths, these will vary from wedding to wedding.

As with a Catholic wedding, the bride and groom will need to have a civil licence for the marriage to be legally recognised. This can be achieved in one of three ways. The couple could have a civil ceremony prior to the religious wedding at a registry office. Alternatively, if either the synagogue's rabbi or secretary are licensed to register marriages, the civil service can be held at the synagogue directly after the religious service. The civil service can also take place in the synagogue after the religious service if a registrar is present to conduct the service.

The best man's role at a Jewish wedding is less involved than in other faiths because many of the duties that are taken up by the male relatives of the bride and groom both before and during the ceremony. Your main role as a source of moral support to the best man remains the same, and you do still have an integral role to play during the ceremony.

The order of procession for the main participants as they enter the church is significantly different to those previously discussed and is as follows:

Rabbi and Cantor (the Rabbi and Cantor will either lead the procession or will enter from a side door and await the wedding party under the *huppah* which is the decorative canopy under which the service is held)

Grandparents of the bride
Grandparents of the groom
Ushers
Groom and his parents
Maid of honour (the equivalent of the chief bridesmaid) and bridesmaids)
Bride and her father and possibly her mother

When the wedding party arrives under the *huppah* the groom stands on the left hand side rather than the right with the best man a step behind him on the left as the bride will take her place on the groom's right. Both the bride's and groom's parents will also stand beneath the *huppah* during the service. Before the bride is allowed under the *huppah* the rabbi will formally ask the groom to name the two witnesses who will sign the marriage document (*ketubah*). These two witnesses should be chosen from outside the families of the bride and groom, so if you are a non-Jewish best man there is every chance that you will be one of the witnesses. The groom is then asked if he accepts the terms of the *ketubah* which details his commitments to his wife. This is followed by the blessings.

The couple are considered to be married under Jewish law once the groom has placed the wedding ring on his bride's finger. This is done by the couple themselves *not* by the rabbi as they are considered to be marrying each other in the presence of the rabbi rather than being married by him. The rabbi is also sometimes chosen as one of the two witnesses to sign the the *ketubah*. The groom places the ring on the bride's right index finger during the service but she will usually transfer it to her left hand once the service is completed.

The *ketubah* is then read in its original form and then in English. It is then presented to the bride and becomes her property as it details her rights within the marriage. After further blessings of the marriage and a prayer for the bride and groom, they sip wine from the same glass to symbolise their shared life together. The groom then breaks the glass. The service concludes with a final blessing from the rabbi.

Non-conformist Weddings
(Methodist, Baptist or Presbyterian)

From the best man's point of view a non-conformist wedding will be very similar to a Church of England wedding. The prevailing customs of the non-conformist churches vary from one to another, but the wedding services are essentially similar, simpler versions of the Church of England ceremony.

As with the other non-Church of England services, a civil licence will be required by the couple, so if the minister is not not licensed to register marriages, a registrar will have to be present at the wedding.

Unless you are yourself a member of the church where the wedding is to be held (in which case you would know all the relevant information) ask the bride and groom how the service differs from the basic Church of England procedures. Some areas to look out for are as follows. Does the church have a central aisle? Many non-conformist churches don't, so you will need to know how this will affect both the seating arrangements and the procession and recession of the bridal party. What will be the accepted etiquette at the reception? Some non-conformist churches take a more formal approach to the after wedding celebrations, so it is possible that there will be no alcohol served and/or you will need to adopt a more serious tone in your speech than otherwise might be expected. When writing the speech, try to find stories which reflect the more exemplary side of the groom's nature rather than the traditional humorous anecdotes.

Civil weddings – registry offices

More and more couples are choosing to get married in registry offices these days. There are a variety of reasons for such a choice – one or both of them may be divorced and unable to marry in church, or they may have no religious beliefs and feel that a church marriage would be hypocritical. Indeed, it is a condition of a registry office wedding that there is no reference to religion in the proceeding, nor can any religious music be played.

Registry offices vary, but civil weddings are by no means spartan affairs. Some registry offices are quite plush and all will provide some flowers to add a bit of traditional wedding ambience to the proceedings.

The ceremony itself is usually a shorter and much more simple affair than that in a church. There are two declarations that the bride and groom must both make for their marriage to be legally recognised. First, that they are legally free to marry:

"I do solemnly declare that I know not of any lawful impediment why I [name] may not be joined in matrimony to [name]."

Second, to call upon those present to witness their marriage vows:

"I call upon these persons here present to witness that I [name] do take [name] to be my lawful wedded husband/wife."

The bride and groom will also be given a choice of vows that they wish to make to one another, or they can choose to write their own, with the stipulation that they can make no religious reference within the vows. It is also a common practice for the bride and groom to ask a friend or relative to give a reading during or at the end of the ceremony, be it a favourite song, poem or something they have written themselves, or the reader has (if you are asked to give such a reading you must remember that it is also not permissible for the reading to be of a religious nature). The readings and the choice of vows helps to give the ceremony a more personalised feel.

There is no legal requirement for an exchange of rings to take place at a registry office wedding, but the vast majority of couples will still want to do so and it is certainly possible for this to be the case.

As with all weddings, there must be at least two witnesses present who will sign the register once the ceremony is complete. At a registry office wedding this will usually be the best man and the chief bridesmaid (if there is one) or the bride's father. However, the choice is the bride's and groom's, so just make sure that you know if you are required to be a signatory.

Once the ceremony is over your duties as best man pretty much mirror those at any other wedding. Make sure that all the guests know where they are going for the reception and that they all have adequate transport to get there. If there are to be official photographs, or if family and friends wish to take their own photographs, this may be done either outside the registry office or at the reception venue (possibly both), depending on the bride's and groom's choice. Again, it is a case of making sure beforehand that you are aware of what the plan is and how you will be expected to help.

Civil weddings – other venues

Since 1995 it has been possible to hold weddings in specially licensed premises such as hotels, stately homes, civic halls, castles and a number of historic buildings. In fact, you can get married just about anywhere you can think of – on a ship, on the beach, or at a sporting arena, for example. More than one couple has been married during the half-time interval at a football match. The style and content of such weddings can vary enormously, and given the size and magnificence of some of the venues now available, it is possible for civil weddings to be even more grandiose than a traditional church wedding.

The reasons for choosing such a venue are often much the same as when a couple opts for a registry office, but the great advantage is that couples can select a venue which reflects their personalities and they are free to tailor the occasion to their own specifications.

The key for any best man at such a wedding, as with any wedding, lies in having all the information at his fingertips. The bride and groom will need to give you a full briefing on the basics such as parking arrangements, seating plan (the majority of venues will attempt to have a traditional seating plan but due to the nature of the venue, or indeed the wishes of the bride and groom, this may not be possible), and most importantly any special considerations that the venue itself may impose, such as asking that ladies do not wear stiletto heeled shoes in order to protect historic flooring. The possibilities here are as varied as the choice of venue, so it really is vital that the bride and groom also appreciate the need for good, solid information if they want you to be able to fulfil your role as best man in the way that both they and you desire.

The service at such venues will be very similar to that in a registry office. The bride and groom must make the two listed declarations and they will have the same options with regard to vows and a reading or music. There will also need to be two witnesses to sign the register.

Weddings abroad

Some couples seeking a more exotic wedding decide to get married in a foreign country. As global travel becomes more accessible and more affordable this is becoming an increasingly popular choice for those who want a truly memorable wedding. Obviously it will fall on the bride and groom to make the vast majority of the arrangements for a wedding abroad, but as best man it will do you no harm to have an overview of the most common areas which need to be addressed when such a wedding is planned.

Most couples who choose to marry abroad will do so through a travel agency which specialises in arranging such events. These companies have specific staff who are dedicated to planning and organising weddings for people who want to have their wedding abroad. They will be able to advise the bride and groom on all the areas which will need to be covered for their chosen destination.

Generally speaking, people are advised to book at least twelve weeks in advance of the wedding date as this allows time for all the arrangements to be made and the appropriate documentation to be completed.

As best man, one of your duties at a more traditional wedding is to ensure that the groom has all the necessary documentation with him on the day of the wedding. At a ceremony held abroad, it is vital that the groom takes all his documents with him as there is no way he can nip back home for anything he has forgotten. If you are travelling out to the wedding destination after the groom it would be a good idea to give him a quick ring after he has arrived to check that he has not left anything behind. If he has, then you can at least pick it up and take it with you when you travel. If you do plan to do this, make sure that you have keys to get in to the groom's house, otherwise you will be unable to retrieve any forgotten documents or other items.

The documentation required by the bride and groom varies from destination to destination, so your best bet is to check with the travel agents exactly what will be needed (if the couple are organising the wedding themselves you could contact the embassy or consulate in the country where the wedding is to be held). Wherever the wedding is being held, the following documents will be needed for the bride and groom:

* Birth certificates
* Current ten-year passport
* Decree absolute (if either party is divorced)
* Previous husband/wife's death certificate (if either party is widowed)
* Parental consent if either party is under eighteen (under twenty-one in some countries)
* Affidavits/statutory declaration confirming single status

(This is a legal document that is obtained from a Commissioner of Oaths, a solicitor who is authorised to validate oaths or statements.)

Couples who choose to marry abroad literally have the world at their feet: the enormous variety of destinations available would take another book to encompass all the possible permutations on offer. As with most areas of a best man's role, the key with overseas weddings is to be organised yourself and to get hold of as much information as possible in advance. In this situation it is particularly important that the bride and groom provide you with as much accurate information as they can. Once abroad, your capacity to sort out any last-minute hitches on the day is significantly reduced.

9
The Best Man's Speech

❧

aking a speech during the reception is the part of the day which most frequently worries anyone asked to be the best man at a wedding. So first bear in mind that you are in good company – if you are feeling nervous about it you are no different from the vast majority of best men. It is also worth remembering the following points.

* The audience you will be addressing is firmly on your side – they want you to make a success of your speech and have a good time as much as you do.

* You will be at least the third speaker so the audience will have been "warmed-up" already. If the speeches preceding yours were not that good, then you will not have to do much to impress the guests and lift the

mood. If, however, the speeches have been witty and amusing, then the audience will already be feeling happy and receptive.

* Everyone will have had at least a little to drink, if only for the toasts already proposed, and will therefore be even more receptive to your speech.

This section of the book will focus entirely on how to write and present the perfect speech to deliver when the time arrives. Sample speeches are scattered throughout this section, and it is followed by a reference section with a selection of quotes, jokes and toasts that you may want to use. You should also feel free to use whole sections of the speeches or even an entire speech if you feel that it is appropriate for the wedding you are attending.

Preparation

The best man's speech is traditionally a light, witty affair, but do not let this fool you into thinking that it will not need a great deal of preparation to ensure that it goes well on the day. Unless you are lucky enough to be someone who makes speeches on a regular basis in your day-to-day life, you will need to learn new set of skills to help you write a suitable speech and then to deliver it fluently and effortlessly. If you stick to the guidelines in the following pages you will not go far wrong and, in fact, you will probably find that despite all your initial misgivings, you will really enjoy the whole performance.

The first thing which you will need to establish when you start to plan your speech is what kind of audience will you be speaking to. If you misjudge the tone and content of your speech you will be greeted by an awkward silence, no matter how good your speech. However, if you get it right there will be joyous laughter and possibly the odd emotional teary eye (not forgetting all those drinks that people will want to buy you as congratulations for doing such a fine job). You should talk to both the bride and groom to establish not only the guests' names, but more importantly, what kind of people they really are. This is because if you only learn basic information such as the names and occupations of the guests you will naturally make your own assumptions about the type of people they are, and these could easily be wide of the mark. Fifty-year-old Aunty Joyce could be anything from a prim and proper regular church-goer, to a maiden aunt with a wicked sense of humour who never settled down. You need to make sure that you entertain the whole audience without offending anyone, and to do this you will need to know as much as possible about your audience, so don't let the bride and groom fob you off with minimal information. All the guests at the wedding will be their family and friends so they should be able to give you a good idea of what will be acceptable. If there is anything which either of them personally asks you not to include, then obviously you must adhere to their request without question, however relevant or funny the anecdote..

SAMPLE SPEECH ONE

This is a speech by a very old friend of the groom, a best man with a long memory who has managed to produce reasonably embarrassing anecdotes.

I'm sure you will all agree that this was a beautiful wedding ceremony – very moving and romantic, just as a wedding should be. My name is Doug and I'm Mike's Best Man. I would like to start by proposing a toast to the bridesmaids – you look stunning and without you, the wedding would not have been the same! I mean you would have had three guys standing off to the right all alone and no one to the left – just kidding.

Well, being Mike's Best Man is indeed a great honour. I remember when he first asked if I would stand up with him – I thought the only problem would be to research and write this speech. While I knew this job came with many other responsibilities, because Mike is so mature and responsible, I expected that finding dirt on him would be hard – WAS I WRONG!

I've heard that the worst five minutes of a man's life is when his Best Man gives the speech. Look at him sweating – Hey Mike, is it too hot in here for you?

I have a huge advantage in that I've known Mike since we were in pre-school together. I remember the day we started first grade. Surprisingly, I was the one who was composed and Mike was a nervous wreck. He really wanted to impress his pretty teacher, trying his best to do everything right. As she led the classroom down the hall toward our room, there was a big yellow sign sitting on the floor where the caretaker had just mopped saying "WET FLOOR". Mike, being the obedient child that he was, did! [Laughter – pause to allow time for the guests to get the joke.]

When we were in the fourth year, Mike was considered by all the teachers to be the perfect student. He was the top of his class in grades and excelled at sports. However, that's not what Mike was best known for around school. Instead, he had several trophies for taking first place in skipping. In fact, he could beat every girl in school. That was quite an accomplishment Mike! In fact, I bet later on, we could talk Mike into giving a sample performance!

Once we got out of school, my family moved to another town and we went our separate ways for a while. When we reconnected in college, our friendship was just as strong as ever. We took holidays together, one summer all over Europe. We had heard about a nudist colony and well, being two young men, we had visions of paradise. One day, we decided to visit the colony, which consisted of people living in tents and tree houses along the beach. Eager to take in the beautiful sight, we walked through dense tree lines, finally coming out into an opening. I will never forget the expression of Mike's face as the first person to greet us was an older man, about 5' 4" tall, and weighing in somewhere around 25 stone! As you can imagine, we didn't stay!

Seriously, Mike has married a lovely woman – Sara. She deserves the best man in the world, but thankfully, Mike got to her first!

I want to thank both of you for choosing this weekend for your wedding and not clashing with next weekend's football opening game. I mean I love you Mike, but it would have been a tough call.

Sara, as you know, I've been friends with Mike for many, many years. We've done some stupid things together, learned many hard life lessons, and enjoyed each other's company. However, during the years as friends, Mike has made some great choices, with the greatest being his marriage to you!

If he had searched the world over, there's no way he would have found to be a better partner in life than you are.

To show our respect and to honour the newly married couple, would everyone please stand with me and raise your glasses.

Mike and Sara, you are a perfect couple and we're all so happy that your lives came together. We wish you a happy future filled with nothing but love and laughter – to Mike and Sara Johnson!

Another way to get a feel for the kind of people who will be in the audience for your speech is to actually speak to some of them. This may seem like an obvious statement to make, but the point here is that you will be able to gauge the type of material you can safely use for your speech, while gathering a wealth of information at the same time.

As best man you will be expected to make a few jokes at the groom's expense and perhaps reveal a few embarrassing stories from his past (remember, though, that while you are expected to get a few laughs at his expense you are *not* there to humiliate him). If you have known the groom for a number of years you will undoubtedly have some funny stories from your times together that you will be able to choose from. The key here is to use stories or anecdotes that demonstrate or exaggerate characteristics of the groom's that most, if not all, of the people in the audience will be able to recognise. By talking to the groom's relatives, other friends, or work colleagues you can find out how they all view him and what kind of person they see him as. We all tend to present different facets of our personality to the different groups of people that we interact with in our lives. What you need to look for are the common threads that run through people's perceptions of the groom which will therefore make the picture that you paint recognisable to everyone.

When you are talking to people ask them for any stories which they may have about the groom. Not only will you be able to get useful material for your speech this way, but it will also make the speech more inclusive of the audience, as any anecdotes from a family member will probably be known by the majority if his family and the same will be true with stories from friends and colleagues. Indeed, you may find that during the speech you end up reminding people of events that they had forgotten about and the memories of these stories will increase their enjoyment of your speech.

Any stories or anecdotes that you can get from people will help you to build up your picture of how the groom is perceived by his friends and relatives. It is important to bear in mind that you will almost definitely end up with far more information than you can use in the actual body of your speech. This is a good thing, as not only is it better to have too much information rather than not enough, but you may also find that while you may not actually use a story recounted to you by someone, it may trigger an idea for another joke or reference which you can use.

An example of this from one of the sample speeches relates to a groom who could fairly be described as a man who occasionally lapses into the odd effeminate gesture or turn of phrase for comic effect. His mother provided a number of stories from his youth, a couple of which were from times when the family would go on caravanning and camping holidays. (See speech on page 112.)

SAMPLE SPEECH TWO

Light, witty and full of anecdotes that will be appreciated by different sections of the audience, this is a finely crafted speech.

Good afternoon ladies and gentlemen, for those of you who don't know me, my name is Steve, and Martin and I have been friends since we were thirteen years old. I stand before you today because, as Martin has finally admitted, and as I've been trying to convince Emma since we met, I am the best man.

I'm sure we can all agree that throughout the day Emma has looked absolutely stunning and that Martin looked . . . Well, like a bloke in a grey suit who's just won the lottery.

Traditionally, this is the part of the proceedings where I stand up and sing the groom's praises. Unfortunately I can't sing and I refuse to lie.

Martin was born on 28th December 1969. The exact location of his birth was a strictly guarded secret until a certain tabloid newspaper published those revelations about a failed government site attempting to end the population explosion by breeding a human so narcissistic that it could only ever love itself.

As a boy Martin spent many happy holidays with his family caravanning in the countryside and he has carried on camping at every opportunity to this very day.

Having completed a charity cycle ride from London to Brighton Martin was being congratulated on his achievement by myself and Keith. "You must be aching all over," we commiserated.

"Oh it's all right", he replied, "I'm used to being saddle sore."

I first met Martin in 1984 when, as teenagers, we were both looking to stand out from the crowd and be different; equally importantly we were looking for other people who were being different in exactly the same way. Ladies and gentlemen, please cast your minds back to the 1980s, the decade that fashion forgot. The make-up, the electric blue hair extensions, the PVC trousers. . . and that was just Martin. One of his proudest buys was a matching belt, T-shirt and baseball cap, all with the word **BOY** written on them. I never did work out whether this was a fashion statement or simply a reminder.

As you can see from the smart grey suit he's wearing today, he maintains his devil-may-care, non-conformist approach to fashion to this very day.

As best man, one of my duties was to ensure that Martin had a good night's sleep before the big day. To this end we simply indulged in a couple of light ales and retired early to bed. Martin duly slept like a baby . . . yep he woke up crying and screaming for his mum every hour . . . oh, and he wet the bed.

Fortunately, I can report that Martin was impeccably behaved on his stag night in Brighton. A special thanks to Brighton resident Keith who managed to lead us in to a bar containing two hen night parties, one dressed as school girls and the other as policewomen, who between them had probably enough material to make one decent skirt. As I say Martin was impeccably behaved, I'm sure due to his overwhelming love and respect, not to say fear, of Emma. That, and considering the state he was in it would have been easier to raise the Titanic.

In the tradition of a number of great romances Martin and Emma were friends long before they became a couple. They first met when they worked together in telesales. No doubt Martin found the years of convincing people that they couldn't live without something that was essentially useless came in handy when he first broached the subject of marriage with Emma.

Over time it became obvious to those of us who know Martin well that his feelings for Emma were more than platonic. It was no surprise to us when they finally decided to declare their love for one another. It is truly rare to see a couple so smitten with one another and so obviously well suited to each other. It is no exaggeration to say that however much fun they are having, both of them light up noticeably when the other enters the room. Their marriage today feels like a happy ending that was destined to be.

It also finally ends Martin's search for a woman who looks better in a dress than he does.

Over the years Martin and I have seen each other through thick and thin, good times and bad, and I can honestly say that I could not wish for a truer friend: he makes me laugh when I need to, provides support when I need it and has helped me learn not to take life too seriously.

If he is half as good a husband to Emma as he has been a friend to me, then they will continue to make each other shine for a very long time. On that note ladies and gentlemen I will ask you all to stand as I propose a toast to two of the finest people I know: to Martin and Emma, the bride and groom.

The various people that you speak to will be able to give insights into the different areas and times of the groom's life. His parents and close relatives should be able to provide you with a wealth of information about what he was like as a child and while he was growing up, which can be a very fertile area for embarrassing stories. We have all done things as children and teenagers that make our adult selves blush at the mere memory and which others will find amusing. Most families have a treasure trove of stories about these early childhood escapades and it's a safe bet the groom's parents will be more than willing to share them with you.

Friends from his adolescence at school and possibly university will be able to shed light on the groom's appalling fashion choices, poor taste in music, his initial experiences with alcohol and his first tentative steps into the world of relationships with the opposite sex. Again, these are the kind of stories which people are usually eager to pass on about their friends and it is a rare person indeed who has not got a closet-full of at least mildly embarrassing skeletons from their teenage years.

Work colleagues, past and present (if you can get in contact with them, should also be able to provide you with some good material about the groom. He may have had an embarrassing misunderstanding on his first day in a new job (more than one person has made a fool of themselves by saying something wholly inappropriate to their new boss on their first day simply because they didn't realise who they were). Remember you are not only looking for amusing stories at his expense (although, granted, this is your major focus), you should also ask people to share stories and reminisce about incidents that demonstrate the admirable side to his personality. In a work situation this could be a time when he has gone out of his way to help a colleague who was struggling with an assignment or was new to the job and just needed someone to take a bit of time to point them in the right direction. The longer you can spend chatting to friends and colleagues, the better your speech will be.

As you gather all these stories about the groom it would be a good idea to keep them all stored in a folder put to one side for the purpose. You will almost certainly be unable to use all the information that you are given, but you will not want to lose any of it and you will need to review it as you go through the process of writing your speech. Try to keep all your notes in one safe place where you have the information easily to hand when you come to start writing the speech.

The order of speeches and toasts

Unless there is to be an official toastmaster at the wedding it is likely that the best man will be asked to fulfil this role in addition to making his own speech. (If this is the case then the best man himself is normally announced by the groom.) Because of this and also because you will need to know what toasts will be proposed by other speakers, you should make sure that you know who all the other speakers at the wedding are to be. It would be a good idea to get in touch with them and clarify the exact running order of the speeches and who is going to propose toasts to whom. It is traditional for the bride's father to toast the happiness of the bride and groom but this is not always the case, and if he does not, then that toast should be proposed by the best man.

The traditional running order of the speeches is: the father of the bride, followed by the groom, who is followed by the best man. These days it is far more common for female participants and the groom's father to make speeches as well, and if this is the case the running order may look this:

> Father of the bride
> Groom
> Bride
> Father of Groom
> Chief Bridesmaid
> Best Man

Exactly how many people will be making a speech will obviously depend on the wishes of the bride and groom, and the running order can be flexible to suit this. It is still generally accepted that however many speakers there are, the father of the bride will speak first and the best man last. The important thing for you to know is the names of all the speakers and in what order they will be speaking.

Traditionally, the father of the bride will welcome all the guests at the start of his speech and then go on to share some endearing and amusing stories of his daughter growing up. He will traditionally end his speech by proposing a toast to the bride and groom's future happiness.

The groom's speech is a more formal affair in which he thanks the bride's father for his kind words and goes on to thank all the attendants for their help in organising and carrying out the wedding. If the bride and groom are presenting gifts to their attendants it is customary for the groom to do so during his speech. The groom will traditionally end his speech with a toast to the bridesmaids. The best man's speech is a response to this toast on behalf of the bridesmaids.

These are the traditional forms for the other two main speeches at a wedding, but as speeches can be a very personal thing, either the bride's father or the groom may choose to vary both the content of their speech and indeed the toast that they propose; it is not uncommon for the groom to propose a toast to his beautiful wife, for example. It is clear that if the groom does not propose a toast to the bridesmaids it would be pointless for you as the best man to open your speech by thanking him for his kind words on their behalf. Likewise if the groom does propose a toast to the bridesmaids, but the chief bridesmaid is also making a speech, it would make more sense for her to thank him for herself and the other bridesmaids. This is why it is vital that you find out who is proposing toasts, as you do not want to either repeat a toast or miss out an important one.

Things to avoid in public speaking

The following would be true wherever you were giving a speech, but they equally apply at weddings.

Never apologise. Unless it's an introduction to a joke apologising about the groom's cheap aftershave, or the haircut he's inflicted on his new bride, don't do it. It doesn't matter if you think you have something to apologise about or not, it deflects attention from what you're going to say. You need to start on a positive note and nothing should be done to detract from that.

If you are feeling nervous, don't go on about it. You may think it will win you sympathy, but the very opposite could happen. People may put up with a few nerves to start with, but listening to a jabbering idiot for ten or fifteen minutes becomes a trial for both speaker and audience. Wedding receptions are possibly the most forgiving audience you could ever have, so enjoy it and don't admit to anything.

Don't step backwards or shrink away from the microphone, if you're using one. For one thing it's poor body language and for another it might be that people won't be able to hear you.

Don't read your speech out. If *The Fear* strikes you deeply whenever you're asked to say a few words, there are ways round the problem (dealt with later in this chapter).

Don't hint that your material might not be exactly new. Okay, so a lot of people have heard of "the key gag" and seen it enacted at weddings, but admitting you knew this already or that you've cobbled together a lot of old jokes is not going to win your audience over.

Never say something like, 'you might be familiar with some of what I am about to say, but bear with me, it gets better, honest!'

Time can stand still when you're delivering a speech and so it's very easy to rush through it. A good way to gauge your pace is by stationing someone you know in a prominent place in the audience. After two minutes make an agreement to look at them and get a "slow down", "speed up" or "just right" hand signal.

SAMPLE SPEECH THREE

This is a warm and sincere speech by the groom's brother-in-law. He has clearly chatted to those who knew the groom as a child, but by and large, has avoided any embarrassing childhood anecdotes, instead enlivening his speech with props and compliments to the bride.

Guests of this wedding, I would like to start today by introducing myself. I am Mike's brother-in-law and his best friend, Joe. Therefore, I was asked to stand up with him today as he and Sara exchanged wedding vows and to give this speech.

Let me first thank each member of the wedding party for their participation in this wedding. Each of you played a crucial role, which resulted in one of the most beautiful weddings I've ever attended.

When Mike asked me to be his Best Man, I was of course honoured, but I immediately questioned his decision-making skills. However, as you can all see, so far everything has gone smoothly. With one of my main responsibilities being to get Mike to the church on time, those of you that know him can appreciate that getting him anywhere on time is a huge challenge.

To Mike's brothers and sisters, mum and dad, if you are worried that I will say something to humiliate Mike, you can relax. Today, I'm only going to be able to speak for a few minutes because of my throat – my wife, Linda, has threatened to slit it if I say anything out of line.

Actually, it is because of Linda that all of you have to listen to me speak today. You see, we met about 18 years ago while on holiday with our families. Since my family is from Newcastle and hers from Sheffield, I spent just about every weekend driving to see her, which is how I met Mike – her brother.

Since I've known Mike for so many years, we are more like brothers than brother-in-laws. In fact, Mike's father, Trevor, actually treats me more like a son, which is why he listed me as a dependent on his tax returns. I think Trevor is still trying to recover some of the costs for feeding and housing me over the years!

To help everyone get to know a little more about Mike, I want to share some of his background. Again, Mike and I met about 18 years ago and although I didn't hang around him when he was a student or early teenager since we lived in different cities, I do know the version of stories that he's chosen to share. My role today is to help you relate to *his* version of events [hold up a very long sheet of paper – about five feet in length].

Mike was an excellent student from what I gather. He had a good rapport with all his teachers and in addition to academics; he is definitely a student of life. He loves researching things to ensure he always makes the right decision. For this reason, you will never see Mike making a quick decision about something he considers important since he believes that the end choices should be made with confidence.

As the Best Man, I've called Mike several times in the last week to make sure he was holding up alright. Just as I expected, he was calm and doing well. I remember when I asked him a few months ago while playing pool how he knew it was time to make the step to sharing his life with Sara. His response was, "I just knew!"

Sara has made a huge impact on Mike's life. I've watched as his personality and behaviour changed, of course for the better. In many ways, Mike is a different person from what he was before he started dating Sara.

Recently, Mike found an interesting article in the newspaper. He shared it with me when he asked me to be his Best Man. Today, I would like everyone here today to listen as

I read it. I honestly believe that for Mike and Sara, it will help them focus on being the husband and wife that they each want and deserve. In fact, every married guest here would benefit from this article.

The story involves a married couple celebrating their Golden Wedding anniversary. Because they had such a loving and strong marriage for 50 years, the local newspaper wanted to interview them so their special secret could be shared with the readers. Their response was as follows:

"Well, the strength of our relationship started on our honeymoon," explained the husband. *"We took a trip to the Grand Canyon in the US, taking a ride to the bottom on a pack mule. We hadn't gone too far down when the mule that my wife was riding, tripped. My wife looked at the mule and with a stern voice she said 'That's once.'"*

As we kept going, the mule again tripped. My wife looked at the mule a second time and said, 'That's twice'. Then, we had only gone about half a mile when for the third time, the mule tripped. Completely frustrated, my wife got off the mule, took a revolver from her purse, and killed the mule – shot him dead between the eyes! Shocked, I started to say something to my wife about her behaviour and in response, she looked at me and said, 'That's once'."

Mike and Sara, although I doubt you will ever have a mule story of your own (at least I hope not), I am confident, along with everyone here, that the two of you will have a special equation that makes your marriage a beautiful success. If everyone will please stand with me and raise your glasses, I would like to offer a toast to the bride and groom as they begin their new life together. We wish that happiness and love will follow you everywhere you go in life.

10
Writing Your Speech

Once you have ascertained the tone of speech that is appropriate for your audience, established who will be speaking and what toasts they will be proposing, and have gathered together a sufficient body of stories and anecdotes from the groom's past you are ready to begin writing your speech.

Before looking at the things you need to do to write a good speech, it would be a good idea to bear in mind some of the things that you should *not* do. You will want everyone to remember your speech for all the right reasons, not because you made a fool of yourself or really humiliated anyone.

Race, religion and politics: There's no need to mention any of them, and if you do, you run the risk of offending someone. However much information you have gathered about the wedding guests, there is no way you can be sure you will be on solid ground with any of these topics so just leave them out.

Past relationships: This applies to the bride's past as well as the groom's. This is their big day as a couple and neither of them will want to be reminded of any previous relationships. They both know all that they have chosen to share with each other about their pasts. It is entirely their business and it would be wholly inappropriate for you to delve into this area on their wedding day. Comic generalisations are fine and there will be some examples of these later, but mentioning specific ex-partners or events in previous relationships would be in very poor taste indeed.

Private jokes: There is no point in making use of any "in" jokes or references that only you and a small number of you friends will understand. Not only will they fail to raise a laugh from the majority of people in the audience, but worse, such anecdotes will probably leave them feeling excluded. Remember ,these people are all on your side when you initially stand up to speak, and that's where you want them to stay.

Swearing: Just don't do it. It really is that simple; you may be able to get away with a clever *double entendre* or two, but outright swearing is guaranteed to offend some, if not all, of the guests, especially if there are children present.

Accent: Many people who are unused to making speeches in public are often tempted to adjust their voices to suit what they regard as a grand occasion, and adopt a falsely posh accent. Avoid this at all costs. You will probably feel uncomfortable with it yourself, and anyone in the audience who knows you will probably be amazed to find the voice of a 1950s BBC announcer coming out of your mouth. Relax and be your self, and the speech will sound all the more sincere for it.

Thank yous: If there is anyone you are supposed to thank in your speech don't forget to do so. If they are expecting to be mentioned then they will be offended if they are not.

Don't rush: If you are nervous about making your speech you may be tempted to try to rush through it to get it over and done with. This a an understandable reaction, but it will lead to disaster, as no-one will be able to follow what you are saying and all your worst fears about making a terrible speech will come true. You will have put a lot of time and effort into preparing both the speech and yourself. Take your time, and speak slowly and clearly so that everyone can hear what you are saying. When you get a laugh, pause until the laughter has died down before you resume speaking.

K.I.S.S.: A wedding is certainly a suitable occasion for kisses. In the case of your speech the K.I.S.S. you should be aiming for is to Keep It Short and Simple. If you ramble on and on you will eventually lose your audience. Between five and ten minutes is ample time to say all that you need to. It is far better to leave the audience wanting more than to have them tapping their feet waiting for you to finish.

Negative feelings: If you have any negative thoughts about the wedding venue, the ceremony, the bride's dress or anything else related to the wedding *keep them to yourself.* This is not your day: it has been organised according to the taste and choice of the bride and groom. Under no circumstances should you make fun of anything.

Don't upset the bride and groom: Be considerate of the fact that this is the bride's and groom's day. Do not do or say anything that may upset either of them. If you are not completely sure about something, then leave it out. It's far better to lose a potentially good joke than to ruin the day and lose a friend.

SAMPLE SPEECH FOUR

Many couples meet at university, and this speech is delivered by a best man who was good friends with both the groom and the bride. A best man in this position stands a greater chance of presenting a really well-balanced speech that incorporates more than just passing complimentary references to the bride.

Before I get too involved with Mike's speech, I should probably introduce myself since many of you don't know me. Those who do, probably wish they didn't. My name is James and I'm Mike's Best Man. Now, I want to let you know right off the bat that the more you laugh at my jokes, the faster the speech will be delivered, so if you're in a hurry to hit the dance floor or start eating, you should laugh!

Being the Best Man takes hard work. In fact, it can be a little nerve-racking. If there's anyone here tonight whose feeling a little apprehensive or nervous about what lies ahead, well, it's probably because you just married Mike! Regardless, I want to take this opportunity not just to destroy Mike's spotless reputation and character, but also to talk about Mike and Sara as a couple.

In 1990, both Mike and I attended [name] University, probably one of the best decisions Mike ever made since that's where he met Sara. From what I remember of that first year, which to be honest isn't a whole lot, he met Sara within weeks and they have been inseparable since.

I remember a bunch of guys in the college would badger Mike, teasing him that he was moving too slowly. I think it took him about a year before he kissed Sara for the first time, but from then on, you knew they were a couple. I mean look at the two of them. Mike met an incredibly beautiful woman who is witty, fun, adventurous, intelligent and in return, Sara got Mike – a balding accountant.

After college, Mike went to work right away for [company name]. He worked so hard and made such an amazing impression on the company that everyone there called him "GOD". Yeah, it was weird – no one ever saw him, he made all the rules, and getting him to do any work was truly a miracle!

Anyway, three years after first meeting Sara, he finally asked her to marry him. At first, I was a little surprised but then I realised that they were clearly meant for one another and they make each other extremely happy!

Okay, so who is the man that Sara has agreed to spend the rest of her life with anyway? He's a great friend who has stood by me through relationship failures and job changes, and is the first person to come to my aid whenever I call. In truth, Mike is the most generous man I know.

I was told that I was supposed to offer Mike and Sara some kind of advice about marriage in this speech, but since I've never been married before and the very prospect of it scares me to death, I won't even try. However, I did take some time to ask some of the married people here tonight what advice they would offer and here's what I found out.

Mike, never be afraid that Sara will leave you. She's invested too much time into training you and it would be devastating to let all that go to waste.

You need to get along exceptionally well with your mother-in-law, which is a huge bonus. In fact, I have a friend that hasn't spoken to his mother-in-law for years simply because he doesn't want to be rude and interrupt her.

Seriously, few Best Men can say that they have been long-time friends of both the bride and groom, so for me, this is a double honour. Although I was terrified when asked to be Mike's Best Man, I wouldn't have turned down the opportunity for anything in the world!

Mike and Sara, I am so confident in your marriage and friendship that I know I'll never again be called to serve as Best Man. This is a one-time shot and I know you will make it an exciting ride all the way. Without doubt, the two of you simply couldn't make it without each other.

I'm proud to call you my friends and proud to be your Best Man. Ladies and gentlemen, would you please stand with me to toast the new Mr. and Mrs. Mike Johnson! May you always have laughter, love, health, and happiness in your life!

Structure

Whatever kind of speech you are going to make, it will be a lot easier to write if you have a structure to work to. In its simplest form, the structure for any speech can be broken down into a beginning, a middle and an end. These basic areas can then be broken down further in a number of ways. Remember that the speech is a personal thing, so while there are some things that you should definitely do and some that you definitely shouldn't, you can play around with the exact nature of the structure and content to make it suit both the occasion and your own personality.

Beginning:

Opening lines

Compliment the bride

Comments on the service

Thanks for any gifts, and or response on behalf of bridesmaids

Middle:

Your relationship with the groom

Stories and anecdotes from the groom's past

Any stories or comments on the stag night (if appropriate!)

Any stories or comments on the bride and groom's romance

Advice to the groom on married life

End:

Praise for the groom

Read any cards or telegrams from people who couldn't make it
to the wedding

Closing lines

Toast

If, from the outset, you know that there are any of the above areas that you are not going to cover in your speech, then you can forget about them and concentrate on the areas that you are planning to expand on. If you are not sure what you are going to include and what you are not (and this is the case with most people when they begin to prepare their speech) then it would be best to plan to include some material on all the areas and then whittle it down when you have a better idea of how your speech is shaping up.

SAMPLE SPEECH FIVE

Beginning with diplomatic, but rather brief thanks to the wedding party, this best man has based his speech on his university friendship with the groom. He has clearly done his research by asking the groom's mother for a couple of stories, too, but has kept his anecdotes jocular without any hint of humiliation.

I would like to start Mike and Sara's wedding reception by introducing myself. My name is Jake and I have had the honour today of serving as Mike's Best Man. I also want to take a minute to thank each member of the wedding party for the amazing job they did in making this a memorable occasion. While the entire bridal party looked stunning, I have to say that no one could outshine the beauty of Sara!

Although I've been told time after time how hard it is to be the Best Man at a wedding, I agreed to stand up with Mike. I thought that the basic roles would not be too difficult to master – you know, getting Mike to the church on time (and sober), making sure he had the rings, his wedding vows, and so on, and I have to admit, it wasn't too bad.

I first met Mike back in 1990 when we attended the same university. Here we were, two macho blokes from different cities, thrown together in one, tiny room. At first,

Mike was very quiet and shy but eventually, with a bit of encouragement, he came out of his shell. I do remember that Mike had a habit of walking around and bumping into things while mumbling under his breath – to look at Mike today, I can honestly say that very little has changed!

Although I didn't know Mike as a kid, I have heard many things about him over the years. The one that stands out is how unselfish he is. For example, he told me that when he was at primary school, he was entered into a sack race one sports day. Apparently, he didn't feel as though he should have won. Therefore, half-way to the finish line, he simply fell over to let a smaller child by the name of Andy win. Wasn't that a nice story, showing just how unselfish Mike is?

Well, his mother has a slightly different version. Does everyone want to hear it? [Wait for a response.] According to Mike's mum, he was involved in a sack race and he was indeed about half-way to the finish line when he fell. However, the race was not lost by Mike because he was giving poor Andy a chance at winning. It was because he had thought that if he could make a little hole in the bottom of the sack to wiggle his foot through, he could get better traction and win. Unfortunately for Mike, his food got all tangled up in the sack, and he tripped over.

On a serious note, one of the obvious aspects of Mike's character is his problem with paranoia. I remember one night when the two of us decided to go out dancing. As we were in the middle of the dance floor, Mike got a very strange look on his face. When I asked him what was wrong, he answered (well, he actually mumbled) that the DJ was staring at him.

It wasn't until I realised that Mike was the only one on the dance floor dancing without a partner that I understood why the DJ was staring so hard. In fact, if you watch him really closely tonight, you'll notice that he leads Sara straight to the corner of the dance floor, well out of the sight of the DJ.

Mike is so fortunate in that he's marrying a wonderful woman – Sara. Not only is she beautiful and kind, but she's one fantastic cook. When we were in college, the only culinary skills Mike had consisted of making toast or heating up beans. No, I take that back – there were a few occasions when Mike would come over all Jamie Oliver by putting cheese on the beans or jam on the toast. Now that I think about it, I do remember one time when Mike decided to put his cooking skills to the test by mixing jam and cheese with his beans and eating it on toast!

In truth, I couldn't have asked for a better friend. Mike has always been there for me, offering the right advice or encouragement when I was down. I hope that I have been half the friend to Mike that he has been to me.

Since Mike is a real romantic at heart, I know that he and Sara will have a loving marriage. When I think of people that should be together, I immediately think of Mike and Sara. The two of you are special and I'm so thrilled that you found each other!

Would everyone please stand and join me in offering a toast to the new Mr and Mrs Mike Johnson. Nothing gets better than this!

Drafting the content

You will already have established what toasts other people will be giving during their speeches, so this should help you to decide which toast or toasts you will propose during your speech. Remember if you are going to propose more than one toast (to the bridesmaids and then to the bride and groom, for example) then you don't have to propose them all at the end of your speech. You can propose one, say to the bridesmaids, during the main body of the speech and the other at the end.

You should also have a wealth of information and stories about the groom and his life which can be used as the basic building blocks for your speech. Initially, all you need to do is to start getting down on paper some rough ideas for things you want to put in your speech. Get a separate piece of paper for each of the headings on pages 136–37 and note down any ideas for each subject. At this stage you are not looking for complete paragraphs or even sentences, unless you come up with something you particularly like and want to make sure that you remember it in its entirety; you are simply looking to note some rough guidelines that you can flesh out later.

Once you are happy that you have enough basic material to build on you can begin to plan your speech more thoroughly. As you begin to flesh out the ideas that you have noted down, you will also be able to start to decide on a more definite structure for your speech to follow. Some stories or jokes will follow each other more naturally than others. Try to be aware of this and ensure that your speech flows from one section to another rather than coming across like several sections bolted together.

Take a fresh sheet of paper and jot down all the points and stories that you have decided to include, in the order that you feel will flow the most easily. This is the basic skeleton of your speech and you are now ready to write the first draft from this structure.

Using the skeleton speech that you have just written as a starting point, write out a complete speech from start to finish, fleshing out all the points you have noted down. Remember that this is only the first draft, so go easy on yourself and don't expect it to be perfect first time around. You will need to spend some time rewriting your speech until you are completely happy with it. Don't expect to be able to do this all in one sitting,. Obviously, you should begin to write the speech several weeks before the wedding to give yourself time to get it just right.

You will find it a lot easier once you have completed your first draft to leave the speech for a day or two at a time and go back to it. This will enable you to mull over anything you are not happy with and come back to it with a fresh mind ready to make the improvements that you feel it needs. It may help if you run through speech in your mind while you are doing other things. Not only will this help you in the process of memorising it, but it may also prompt a few improvements. The more relaxed you are when mulling over your speech, the better your creative juices will flow. The pressure of an imminent deadline (the wedding day) may focus your mind on finishing the speech, but it is really best if you can add the final polish in your own time. If you feel it would help, you could carry a small notebook and pen around with you so that you can note down any ideas that come to you in idle moments. You may even find that you do not complete the first draft in one go. This is perfectly alright: if you are really struggling leave it for a while and come back to it later, as it will be better to approach things once you feel refreshed and have a clear head to think it all through.

One very important point to bear in mind is that your speech is a spoken piece of communication and not a written one. When you first begin to write down ideas, you will naturally do so in an essay-like fashion and this is fine to begin with as you are only trying to get the basic ideas down on paper. As you begin to rewrite the original draft it is a good idea to speak it out loud as you run through it, as this will help you to identify any areas that you are uncomfortable with. Any parts of the speech which sound awkward when read out loud must be rewritten in a more conversational manner so that you are happy with the way it sounds. It will also make the speech more pleasurable for the audience to listen to. Remember that they will be expecting an amusing speech, not a lecture.

There are some best men for whom the fear of public speaking is just so great that they decide to produce an exact script – they write out the speech in full and bury their heads in the document as they read it out. And it sounds awful. The sense of occasion is totally lost with a written speech and leaves you no freedom to adjust to good-natured hecklers as you go along. If the fear is just too great, then the one thing you can do is produce a speech that mimics the flow of the written word. For instance you could read out a fictional report from the groom's school, a dire reference from his boss, a letter supposedly sent from an anonymous member of the bride's family to the bride begging her to think again before it's too late.

Armed with the confidence that this will give you, it should be possible to link to some more written material, throw in a few sincere remarks and end with a joke or an anecdote that you've learned.

Opening lines

The opening lines of your speech are probably the most important part of your speech as they will set the tone for what is to follow. Ideally, you want something that will grab the audience's attention right from the start. It is also a good idea to introduce yourself to the audience right at the beginning of your speech as it is quite likely that a number of them will not know who you are and this will help to warm them to you. There are two main types of opening lines that you can choose from, either a joke to get everyone laughing right away, or try a rather more sincere introduction. Which of these opening styles you choose is entirely up to you and will depend on what you feel most comfortable with and what kind of wedding you are attending. Either way, you should make sure that you are entirely happy with your opening lines and you know them inside out. Spend a little extra time on this part of your speech to ensure that you create exactly the kind of first impression that you want.

Compare the following two speeches.

SAMPLE SPEECH SIX

This speech begins with an immediate joke to get the audience warmed up. Note that the joke has nothing to do with the groom or the wedding. The speech is peppered with a series of quips at the groom's expense, and is slightly disjointed because the subject matter does not always flow seamlessly.

Well, the moment has finally arrived for a little character assassination. My name is David Smith and as the Best Man, it is my honour and opportunity to comply . . . although, as Henry the Eighth told one of his wives, "I won't keep you long." Considering that I have never done this before, I am not sure exactly how long my speech will last so if I notice too many of you nodding off, I'll try to take that as a hint!

When Mike asked me if I would be the Best Man at his wedding, I was thrilled and jumped at the chance. All of the speech books I could get my hands on said that I should not just slate him but that I needed to tell you a little something about him – and mention his good points too!

Mike was born in the same year that the first Kodak Instamatic camera was made, the British decimal coins were produced, the Boeing 747 and the Concorde made their first flights, test-tube fertilisation of human eggs was performed, and scientists created the epidural injection to help with painful childbirth – very interesting, wouldn't you agree?

Although Mike finished secondary school and even went on to college, he was not necessarily regarded as the brightest student in class. In fact, one day, we decided to go out for pepperoni pizza, his all-time favourite. When the waiter asked if he wanted it cut in four or eight slices, do you know what he said? "Cut it into four: I don't think I could eat all eight."

To give you a better idea of what Mike was like at school, I conned his mother into lending me some of his old reports. One of them reads, "Mike is an *ideal* student that *excelled* in all his subjects." That's great, right. Well, as I looked a little closer, I noticed that the report had been doctored (probably by Mike) and that it actually reads, "Mike is an *idle* student that was *expelled* from all his subjects!"

Okay, enough talk about school. Mike is a wonderful individual who *could* be described as handsome, entertaining, intelligent, and of course, charming – and perhaps one day he will be.

Seriously, Mike is successful, highly intellectual, witty, and … hey Mike, what else did you write here? I'm having trouble reading your handwriting!

Most of you are probably aware of how infuriating Mike can be. He always seems to show up late or simply doesn't show up at all. I mean, he leaves everything to the very last minute such as organising his wedding in two weeks! Now I love Mike but to give you an idea, just last week, I was sent a flyer advising that the people Mike has known for years are now forming support groups.

Mike has also been said to be naïve, but I didn't agree with that at first. From what I could tell, he was very wise. However, now that he has asked me to be his Best Man and give this speech, I can see why people said that.

Honestly, marriage is a beautiful thing. It teaches two people about compromise, loyalty, and trust. I'm confident that marriage will transform Mike into a magnificent husband and endow him with other qualities that might not have been discovered if he had chosen to stay single.

In fact, when I asked Mike what is was he was looking for in his marriage to Sara, he told me happiness, love, and someday, little ones running around the house. The funny thing is, when I asked Sara the same question, she said, "A good blender and someone to cut the grass".

Well, my speech is actually almost done but before I finish, would everyone please stand and join me in offering a toast to Mike and Sara, two wonderful, loving people who, without each other, wouldn't be the same.

From the bottom of my heart, and with all kidding aside, may your love survive the test of time, and last forever. Each of us in this room wishes you a long life of love, laughter, and growth. Along with the good times, there will be tough times but I am confident that together you will get through whatever hand life deals.

I propose a toast in honour of your marriage, wishing you nothing but good things. Please raise your glasses with me, as I congratulate the new Mr and Mrs Mike Johnson!

SAMPLE SPEECH SEVEN

This warm and sincere speech has a rather self-deprecating start, and includes fulsome thanks to the wedding party, who will probably feel really pleased to be singled out for praise. The anecdotes about the groom are kept to a minimum in exchange for some amusing advice.

Good evening everyone and for guests that have no idea who I am, my name is David and unfortunately for you, today I'm Mike Johnson's Best Man. First, I want to extend my thanks to Debbie, Jenna, and Martha, three wonderful and beautiful bridesmaids and Nancy, an amazing Maid of Honour!

I also want to thank the ushers who worked so hard in getting everyone seated and organised: Dennis and James – thank you. Additionally, I want to extend a note of gratitude to the groomsmen, Jeff, Carl, and Pete for supporting me over the past several months and doing such a wonderful job today. Most importantly, I want to sincerely thank the bride and groom for being here and allowing all of us to share in this incredibly special day.

Going by tradition, the Best Man is supposed to dig up embarrassing stories about the groom's past, sort of carrying out a character assassination, but because I have such immense respect for this man, I'm afraid I just can't do that. I mean for me to mention the time he streaked across the high school stage during the performance of *Annie Get Your Gun*, wearing only a gun holster would be mortifying.

I would no more tell you about the time he dressed up as a woman for Hallowe'en or about the time he was so drunk he got up to sing an entire rendition of *Somewhere over the Rainbow* during a Karaoke contest…and won – oh wait, what am I thinking?

That's enough about Mike. As I spoke with various guests here tonight, I took notes from those that had been married for years and years. They were easy to spot: standing next to each other in complete silence. I gathered as much advice on the ingredients for a happy and successful marriage as I could. Mike, here is what the people wanted to tell you:

You need to establish that you're the boss, the king of your castle, but just be sure you do exactly what Sara tells you.

Never forget the five rings of marriage:

Engagement RING

Wedding RING

SuffeRING

TortuRING

EnduRING

Just remember, Mike, marriage is not just an eight-letter word. It's an entire sentence – although in most countries, you would probably get much less for murder! Another piece of advice is that is the best way to remember your wedding anniversary is to forget it … just once. Okay, seriously, my best advice to you is always remember three simple words – "You're right Sara!"

You will all be happy to know that I just have a few more things to say … in all seriousness, Mike, it has been an honour and privilege to serve as your Best Man today. You are a very fortunate man to have met such a wonderful woman as Sara. She is caring, loving, smart, and the perfect match for you any day of the week. For you Sara, you found … well, Mike!

The two of you will have a healthy and loving marriage and I'm thrilled to call you both my friends. Finally, it gives me great pleasure to invite all of you to stand, raise your glasses to the newly married couple, and join me in wishing them good health and a wonderful life together. Here's to you Mike and Sara!

Prompt cards

Even if you are confident that you will be able to remember the whole of your speech on the wedding day, it is a good idea to prepare some prompt cards, just in case. Whatever you do, you should *not* stand up with a full copy of the speech to read from. It will act as a barrier between you and the audience, and if you are nervous it will not help, for two very good reasons. First, you could be tempted to keep your head down and read the whole speech from the script in front of you (this is a definite no-no as the audience will not feel at all engaged if you do so), and second, if you do lose your place and forget a line it will take too long to find it again.

What you need are bullet points to trigger your memory for each section of the the speech. As an example look at the following paragraph from one of the speech on page 112.

"Martin was born on 28th December1969. The exact location of his birth was a strictly guarded secret until a certain tabloid newspaper published those revelations about a failed government site attempting to end the population explosion by breeding a human so narcissistic that it could only ever love itself. As a boy Martin spent many happy holidays with his family caravanning in the countryside and he has carried on camping at every opportunity to this very day."

On a prompt card the above two paragraphs could be summed up as *Birthday revelations and Camping.*

By the time you actually make your speech you should be familiar enough with the content that you only need a small mental nudge to get you back on track should you forget anything. What is important is that you use words or short phrases that will trigger *your* memory. As you begin to practice reading out your speech, you will find that certain key words or phrases stick in your mind, and these are the ones to use on your prompt cards.

SAMPLE SPEECH EIGHT

After thanking the groom on behalf of the bridesmaids, a slightly nervous beginning gives way to a well-constructed speech. This best man manages to convey his real affection for the groom, as well as his admiration for his friend's choice of bride.

First, on behalf of the Maid of Honour and bridesmaids, thank you Mike for your kind words. Each of you look beautiful and added a touch of magic to this very special day.

My name is Jeff and I'm Mike's closest friend and Best Man. I tried hard to memorise the speech and will do the best I can, but don't be surprised if I refer to my cue cards every five seconds!

Let me start by saying that Mike and I met twelve years ago while we were both going through what our teachers referred to as "the teen phase". We both attended a private school, which was a laugh! I remember the teachers always thought the two of us were so admirable because we would volunteer to clean up in the kitchen after every Friday's lunch. Little did they know that the only reason we did that was because we had figured out that that was the day the chocolate machine man brought the new boxes of Mars bars – and left them absolutely unguarded!

No matter what has happened in my life, Mike has been there for me. For instance, when I lost control and wrecked my new Cortina, Mike was there. When my girlfriend of two years dumped me for someone else, Mike was there. When I lost my job, Mike was there. Now that I think about it, I think Mike jinxed me!

In all the years I've known Mike, he has been so kind in giving me an endless supply of ammunition in preparation for this very day. Little did he know that I have been taking notes for the past twelve years!

When I was asked to be his Best Man, I was given a few topics that I should not discuss – no matter what! No problem – I'm happy to bypass his stories and just share mine. Let me tell you about one Christmas when I went to visit Mike in Brighton. He had moved there and decided while visiting that we should do something constructive instead of just drinking. As you can imagine, we were both very confused on how to start, so we went to a pub and grabbed a couple of pints to talk about our big plans.

Mike's big idea was that we should go water-skiing. Now, since neither one of us had tried this before, I can't say this was one of his better ideas but I decided to go along. We got on the internet and read everything we could about water-skiing and even made a trip to the library. Well, as you can imagine, the trip was a disaster. Saying that we spent a day ON the water should have been changed to spending a day UNDER water. I don't think either one of us ever got up on the skis.

I apologise for the next memory – you had to be there to relish full comedic effect – but it does sum up Mike's doggedness and determination and its inevitably disastrous consequences. We were going to a gig at the [name] Hall. I don't even remember the name of the band: all we knew was there would be women inside. When got there, it was sold out. So did we give up and go for a drink? Oh no, not with Mike in the party! He reckoned if we went up ON THE ROOF he knew a way to get in through the skylight. Amazingly, we did it, only to fiind ourselves backstage! Undaunted, Mike strode confidently past the bemused drummer towards the dance floor. Dazzled either by the spotlights or the sight of so many representatives of the opposite sex in one room, the last thing I saw of Mike was his Martin Fry cowlick of blonde hair standing straight up as he plunged off the stage into complete darkness and the arms of a rhino-size bouncer.

That's the great thing about Mike – he'll always take a dare, which is exactly how he met Sara. She was sitting alone eating lunch on campus when I dared him to go over and strike up a conversation. Of course, he did and well, here we are today! Mike was always coming up with brainy ideas but I have to admit the best one was in asking Sara to be his wife. Mike, I'm proud of you for making the best decision of your life and I wish the two of you all the happiness in the world.

Ladies and gentlemen, would you please join me in standing, as we raise our glasses to offer a heartfelt toast to the newly married couple – Mike and Sara Johnson.

Games, stunts and props

If you feel comfortable doing so, a great way to liven up your speech and make it more memorable is to incorporate a game, stunt or prop into the proceedings. One of the great advantages of doing this is that involves the audience in your speech, which will make them even more appreciative of it.

Some examples that you may like to try are listed below, or if you are feeling particularly adventurous you may like to think of an original one of your own.

Scrapbook: When you are doing the research for your speech ask people if they have any photographs of the groom that you could borrow, the more embarrassing the better. Bear in mind, though, that they will be shown to all his family. If there are any particularly lewd photographs it would be wise not to include these. Make sure that you know which photographs you have borrowed from whom, as if you fail to return them it may well lead to bad feelings. Better still, get copies printed.

The idea here is to make up an amusing scrapbook showing the groom from his first days as a bouncing baby through his childhood and teenage years, up to the present day. You could also include a selection of juvenilia, such as examples of the groom's handwriting as a child, or pictures he drew, maybe even copies of his old school reports.

Ideally, you should try to copy all of the items that you want to include in the scrapbook and make an identical scrapbook for each table at the wedding reception. If this is not possible and you can only make one copy you could leave it on the nearest table to the entrance with a note asking the guests to read it and then pass it along to the next table.

It can be particularly good if you refer to something in the scrapbook in the body of your speech. The sample speech on page 115 contains a sentimental line followed by a joke which refers to a photograph of the groom taken at a fancy dress party which he attended dressed as Marilyn Monroe.

"Emma and Martin's wedding today feels like a happy day that was destined to be. It also finally ends Martin's search for a woman who looks better in a dress than he does." If you can tie in the contents of the scrapbook with the contents of your speech, it makes it more memorable but is not absolutely necessary. A scrapbook will be fondly remembered by many of the guests for a long time to come.

Slideshow: This is a variation on the scrapbook idea. Rather than putting together a scrapbook of the groom's life from photographs. if you have facilities to make slides out of the photographs that you borrow from his friends and family you can put together a slideshow of his life. You could also use a laptop computer and produce a slideshow presentation on that. Obviously this will be more time-consuming and take a lot more planning. You will need to make sure that the reception venue has the facilities to enable you to show your slideshow. However if you can do so, it will look truly impressive and you could choose to build your entire speech around the slideshow and presentation.

If you do choose to present a slideshow as part of your speech, you would be well advised to contact the reception venue to arrange an opportunity to have a practice run-through prior to the wedding. Not only will this give you the chance to familiarise yourself with the equipment you will be using on the day, it will also avoid major disappointment if you turn up on the day are unable to run the slides.

SAMPLE SPEECH NINE

After a tentative start, this best man proves he is a natural entertainer by using a few props with aplomb and incorporating some amusing telegrams from celebrity "friends" of the happy couple.

Good evening ladies and gentlemen. My name is Gerald and I'm Mike's Best Man. To be honest, I'm just as nervous as Mike was this morning, but I'll do my very best not to make too much of a mess of this speech.

First, on behalf of Mike and Sara, all of the wedding party has done a beautiful job today, making this the fairy tale wedding they have both always dreamed of having.

A little bit about me. I have known Mike for the past 16 years. During that time, we have laughed, cried, worked, and been embarrassed. In fact, one of the most embarrassing times of my life was one night when Mike and I were out dancing at one of the hottest, most electrifying night-clubs around. Okay, so you might be asking what is so embarrassing about that. Well, when you see Mike out on the dance floor later tonight, you'll understand!

With tradition, the Best Man is supposed to offer a toast to the groom and include in his speech some comments that would focus on his faults [pull out a stack of cards about four inches thick]. While I could not possibly go through each and every one of these, [fan them out for exaggeration] especially since there are about six stories per page, I will do my best to keep you entertained.

Although Mike is certainly a smart man, he has his moments. For instance, he thought that Alfred Hitchcock was some brand of jockstrap. Despite his shortcomings, Mike does pretty well. One night in particular, Mike and I, along with a mutual friend, Steve, were walking home having been out drinking. Tired from walking, we stopped and were leaning against a building just waiting – for what, I'm not sure. Within minutes, a police officer walked over to us, asking what we were doing and then asked for our names. Since we didn't want to get into trouble, I started by giving him a bogus name (like that was not going to get us into trouble).

Feeling confident that Mike and Steve would notice what I did and follow, I stated my name was Grant Spencer. Without hesitation, Steve followed my lead, giving the officer the name of David James. Finally, it was Mike's turn. Looking at us and winking to let us know he understood what we were doing, he blurted out that his name was Ken. When the officer asked for his last name, Mike fumbled, finally coming up with the last name of "*Tuckyfriedchicken*". Well, needless to say, we spent the night on a cold, hard bench going through detox!

To be honest, I was shocked when Mike told me that he had asked Sara to marry him but knowing how loyal and hard-working he is, I knew he would make a great husband. In fact, I brought some pictures today to show you how hard working Mike is [with a projector and slides].

This first picture shows Mike helping his mum in the garden [picture of Mike lying on the lawn asleep]. The second picture shows Mike as he spends time working with his father on the family car [picture of Mike asleep in the front seat]. Finally, this last picture was taken of Mike while planning this wedding [picture of Mike asleep on the couch].

Today, I'm glad to see Mike letting his hair down a little, especially since his hair has been letting him down for the past year. However, Mike I've heard that there are some excellent new products and procedures on the market. What makes these products so unique is that they don't actually help hair to grow, but instead, they help to shrink your head so that your hair fits better.

I know that Mike and Sara would like to thank those of you here that have travelled great distances to share in this memorable day. Some of the individuals unable to attend have sent telegrams and I would like to take a minute to read a couple of messages to the bride and groom.

To Sara – *We could have been so great together* – With special love from Brad Pitt.

To Mike – *Sorry we weren't able to attend your wedding, especially the reception, in that we have so much the Best Man could have used in his speech! Regardless, Sara, if you ever need any ammunition, just call.* Love, the Jones's.

Seriously, it gives me great pleasure to invite each of you to stand and raise your glasses, as we toast the new couple – Mr. and Mrs Mike Johnson. You are truly an amazing couple and every person in this room is so happy that you found one another to share your lives.

Limericks: Put a small card and a pen or pencil for every guest on all the tables and a note asking them to write a limerick about the groom (or the bride as some of the guests may not know the groom). After the main course of the meal gather up all the limericks that have been written and spend some time during the dessert reading through them and choosing a few of the most amusing ones to read out during your speech. You may want to enlist the help of the ushers in collecting and vetting the limericks as this will leave you with more time to be sociable during the meal.

This will work really well if you ask people to put their names on the cards as you can mention who has written the limericks before you read them out. You will be guaranteed to get a cheer from the table of anyone whose limerick you read out.

Mr and Mrs: This can provide an opportunity for all the guests to get to know a bit more about the bride and groom as well as enjoy a bit of a laugh at their expense. Put together a list of questions about the couple and their relationship. Remember to include questions about all the different stages and aspects of their lives, as this will give everyone present a chance to get some of the questions right. It is also a good idea to make some of the questions loaded to provide amusing answers at the expense of the couple (as with everything though, mild embarrassment is good but anything more will be in bad taste). Leave a copy of the questions on each table along with a pen for people to write down their answers.

This is also a great icebreaker for people who are sharing a table with other guests who they don't know very well. As any bride and groom will be able to tell you, the seating plan for the reception is always a headache and you will always end up seating some people together who have not met before.

You can choose when to go through the answers. You can either do it as part of your speech, or at the beginning or end of all the speeches.

Simply ask the tables to swap their answer sheets and mark each other's answers. If you are feeling generous you could offer a bottle of wine or champagne to the table with the most right answers.

Sweepstake: Organise a sweepstake on the total time that the speeches will take. Find out how many guests there will be and create small tickets with a range of times on them. You can either ask the ushers to hand out the tickets as guests arrive at the reception, or leave them on the tables.

Make sure that the chief usher or the father of the bride has a stopwatch and that they don't forget to start and stop the timer as the speeches begin and end. The person with the closest ticket to the correct time wins.

Whether you choose to ask people to pay a small amount for their tickets (obviously you need to get the ushers to sell the tickets as people arrive if you do this) and use the money for a prize (or give it as a gift to the bride and groom) or to give out a bottle is up to you.

The key gag: This is one that will take a bit of arranging to organise but can be really funny if it is pulled off well. The easiest way to organise it is to brief as many of the female guests in advance of the wedding of what you require them to do. If you are unable to do this you could enlist the help of the ushers and get them to speak to all the female guests at a discreet moment before the speeches start. You need to keep this manoeuvre a secret from the groom and as many of the male guests as possible for it to have maximum effect, and you should make sure that everyone asked to participate is also aware of this fact.

During your speech allude to the groom's bachelor days and how disappointed all the women in the world will be that he has found the woman of his dreams and is therefore unavailable. You then ask anyone who still has a key to his house or flat to please return it to the top table. At this point hordes of women make their way to the top table carrying keys.

This works well because it is an obvious joke and can in no way be deemed to be a genuine reference to the groom's real past life as a "man about town". There are only two things to be wary of: if the groom genuinely does have a chequered past and this is a sore point with the bride, or if there are any of his ex-partners in the room, it would probably be more tactful not to use the key gag. *Warning*: unfortunately, this gag has now been distributed widely on the internet, so it may be getting too well known.

Presents: There are a couple of different jokes you can use by giving presents to the bride and groom.

Russian doll: At the start of your speech present the bride with a large, gift-wrapped box and ask her to open her present. As she unwraps each layer of the present it reveals a smaller box until eventually she opens a tiny box with a note inside. The note will say that you are really sorry, but you couldn't think of anything to say in your speech, and then thanks her for helping to pad out the time for you.

Honeymoon kit: Present the groom with a honeymoon kit containing humorous items such as bandages, whips, viagra, a feather duster, etc.

School report: You can either try to get some genuine old school reports from the groom's parents, or simply write a completely fake one yourself. Read extracts out as part of your speech and link them to the groom's present day life. For example, "Mr. Jones the woodwork teacher noted in 1987 that 'John does not pay due attention to the instructions that he is given and struggles to use his tools in the correct manner.' I sincerely hope for Jane's sake that he has learnt from his youth and is not still plagued by these problems."

SAMPLE SPEECH TEN

Asking your younger brother to be best man shows an incredible amount of trust on the part of the groom. This speech incorporates an array of jokes, uses school reports for extra humour, and finishes with a rather touching tribute to the newly-weds.

Hello – I'm David, Mike's younger brother and his Best Man. Today, I have the honour of sharing with you for a few minutes. First, on behalf of the bridesmaids and flower girls, I want to thank Mike for his kind words. Everyone today did an incredible job and looked amazing, especially Sara.

When Mike asked if I would stand up with him as best man, he gave me a long running list of things I shouldn't mention. For some reason, memories of our childhood came racing to my mind, giving me the opportunity to get revenge for all the years of emotional and physical torment at his hands. Well, while I appreciate your request Mike, but unfortunately for you, Sara gave me artistic freedom (and a guaranteed dinner every Sunday) to say whatever I like.

Interestingly, Mike thinks of his existence as being glorified. He thinks his life story would make an excellent televised autobiography or drama. To support his belief, it would only be fair as his Best Man and brother, that I pay tribute to his life by providing you with a little bit of history:

Mike was born in 1969.

He left school in 1987.

He started working for (company name) in 1988.

Mike met Sara in 1990.

Mike and Sara were married today.

Yep, I would say that is powerful enough to be dramatised on television!

Mike remembers his schools years in detail, especially how he excelled at everything that he did. I thought it would be nice to get a copy of some of his reports to share all the wonderful things the teachers had to say:

History – Mr Baxter – While Mike tries very hard in class, since the last report, he has now reached rock bottom.

Economics – Ms Wilson – I am convinced that Mike can go very far in life – the sooner he gets started, the better.

Science – Mrs Miller – Although Mike is very enthusiastic, I have concluded that if brains were taxed, his would receive a rebate.

The famous Andy Warhol once stated – "In the future, everyone in the world will be famous for 15 minutes". I believe Mike's 15 minutes came in 1979 at the age of 10 when we went to a school football game with our father. His picture and a short story were featured on the front page of the local newspaper. The story proceeded to tell readers how several police officers and firemen spent hours searching for him only to discover that he had climbed on top of the score-board where he was stranded and had to be rescued.

I was asked a few months ago if I looked up to Mike as my big brother. For about two seconds, I gave it some thought. Then without hesitation, I replied that Mike was more a source of perspiration than inspiration. That doesn't mean that Mike never made an impression on me – just look at the three-inch scar left on my forehead, or the permanent footprint left on my back – those flippin' football studs!

The funny thing is that Mike was given the nickname of "short straw" by friends since he seems to have the uncanny ability always to draw the short end of the deal. However, when he found Sara, he certainly didn't get the short straw that day. Instead, he met a beautiful woman who is warm and charming, and somehow, she loves my brother in spite of his shortcomings.

Before we toast the newly married couple, I wanted to read a few messages from close friends and family members who were not able to be here today.

From Keith (a close friend from an old job) – *Hullo Mike and Sara – I'm really sorry that I wasn't there to celebrate your wedding today but I wasn't invited!*

From Danny (his old boss) – *We found Mike to be worthless in every position – Sara, we hope you have better luck!*

I want to thank Mike and Sara's parents for doing such an incredible job in raising their children. In my wildest imagination, I could never have imagined that two terrific people such as this would find each other to share their lives. Mike, I also want to thank you for giving me the honour of being your Best Man today. I'm proud of you as my friend and as my brother. With all sincerity, I wish you and Sara a lifetime of happiness.

With that said, would everyone please stand with me, raise your glasses, and let's salute the new Mr and Mrs Mike Johnson. We all wish you well for the future and hope you enjoy a long and happy marriage!

SAMPLE SPEECH ELEVEN

The groom's older brother is the best man here, and after a gracious vote of thanks to those who helped organise the wedding, he assumes the air of a game show host. This is a confident speech full of well-timed jokes where sincerity and love are balanced by brotherly good humour.

Good evening ladies and gentlemen. For those that have no idea who I am, my name is Les and I'm Mike's Best Man, but this is just a nominal title, since I'm also his older brother. To begin, on behalf of the Maid of Honour, Debbie, the bridesmaids, Lesley, Shannon, and Lisa, and the groomsmen, Vince, Russell, and Tim, thank you for the beautiful job you did tonight. The wedding would simply not have been the same without your presence.

I also want to thank both Mike and Sara's parents. I know you have all worked feverishly over the past months to ensure this day was perfect. Believe me, you should have seen them during the wedding rehearsal.

Additionally, a big thank you goes out to everyone who pulled together in organising today's wedding: it was a huge amount of work but I'm sure everyone will agree that the results are magnificent.

Most importantly, thank you Mike for allowing me to stand with you as your Best Man. I appreciate this special honour – and for making me a nervous wreck! When Mike first asked me to be his Best Man, I was so excited, thinking "What a great honour," but that was soon followed by the thought, "What have I done recenlty that Mike is getting even for?"

I remember specifically Mike telling me not to worry, and that he had a book I could borrow. Good going Mike – you obviously didn't read it. When I reached page 14, I read, *Maintaining a clear head during the wedding celebrations is vital for the Best Man.* However, not quite sure what this meant, I continued reading when I finally reached page 60. Here's what I found out that I was supposed to do:

Help the groom get dressed – Well, if Mike hasn't learned how to do that by himself at his age, I'm certainly not going to start helping him now.

Ensure the groom uses the toilet prior to walking down the aisle – you've got to be kidding!

Make sure the groom has his shoes tied, his hair in place, nothing on his face, there is nothing between his teeth or in his ears, and his flies is up – Oh dear! I mean I love Mike, but these instructions are pushing it…

During the speech, I am supposed to introduce the guests to the groom. While some of you probably know him quite well, some of you may not know much about Mike's background. Well, the speech is supposed to give me the opportunity to demolish Mike's character, probably in return for my checking his teeth, flies, and all those other fun things. Personally, I don't see any reason why this speech should break that rule. In fact, assassination of character makes it all the more fun, especially now that Sara has married him and it's too late to back out.

When Mike handed me the Best Man speech book, he also gave me a list of stipulations to ensure that the speech was not crude, rude, or embarrassing – what was he thinking? I mean did he really think I was going to follow that. Just look at Mike – do you see the little beads of sweat forming on his forehead? That, my friend, is what you call nerves! Of course, I suppose if I were in his place, I would worry about the Best Man revealing skeletons in my closet too.

Well, although I know it's hard to imagine, Mike is not perfect. Before I get into the fun part of the speech, I need each of you to help me out. Is everyone game? [wait for a response]. I didn't hear you – a little louder please [again, wait for a response]. Great. Let's start by having everyone scoot up on the edge of your seat – just don't fall off. I need everyone in the room to participate.

For the guests sitting on the right side of the room, you will respond with a nice, loud, OOH and everyone from the left side, AHH. Got it? Okay, so what's the purpose of this? Well, I told Mike very specifically that the only way I would give this speech is if all the guests oohed and ahhed while sitting on the edge of their seats!

When Mike was a little boy, he was the perfect child. Seriously, he was seldom naughty, very nice, considerate, and extremely gifted. In school, Mike was popular and did very well in everything, whether it was academics, arts, or sports. The only vice I'm aware of during his school days was the collection of bogies he had behind his headboard, which would not be discovered for months after he moved out. [Pause for laughter and groans.]

Mike, you are an incredibly lucky groom in that you snagged Sara. As everyone can see, she is stunning, warm, loving, caring, and smart. In return, she married a man with unique interests and talents. Sara, just keep an eye on the back of your headboard!

Seriously, Mike will make a loving and thoughtful husband and the two of you will have a wonderful life together. Will everyone please stand with me to raise your glass in a toast to the newly married couple?

To Mike and Sara, everyone in this room extends heartfelt congratulations on your marriage. We know that the two of you were made for each other and we couldn't be happier for you. To your life, may it be filled with joy, adventure, and lots of love!

If all else fails and you're totally stuck for inspiration when it comes to writing a speech, don't despair. There are people you can turn to for help. The publishers would like to thank Dan Stevens at www.weddingspeech4u.com for supplying many of the sample speeches that appear in this chapter. This excellent site also features professionally written and inspiring speeches for the father of the bride and maids of honour.

11
Delivering the Speech

N ow that you have written your speech you need to practice actually delivering it. It is important to understand that while *what* you say is important, (and that is exactly why you have gone to all that trouble to write the perfect speech), *how* you say it is equally important. Someone could stand up with the best speech in the world, but if they deliver it in a consistently dull monotone, it will have the audience bored in seconds. Conversely, an average speech can be made to sound good by a person who stands up and injects it with genuine passion and emotion.

Relax

The first thing that you need to do to ensure that you do justice to the speech you have worked so hard to prepare is to make sure that you are as relaxed as possible when you stand up to make it. There are four steps that you can take to make sure that this is the case.

1. Try to empty your mind of all thoughts. This may seem like an impossible thing to do if your mind is concerned with all the things that could go wrong, but if you concentrate on your breathing you should be able to manage it. Take a deep breath through your nose and fill you're your lungs with air, now hold your breath for a couple of seconds and then breath out slowly and fully through your mouth. If you do this three or four times it should help to relax you and if you can concentrate on the actions of your breathing it will clear your mind of unwanted negative thoughts.

2. Contract your stomach muscles as tight as you can and then relax them. Clench your hands into fists as tight as you can (without digging your nails into the palm of your hand) and then relax. Extend your fingers in as wide a span as you can and then relax. Push your arms tightly into your side and then relax. Lastly, press your feet firmly into the floor and then relax them.

3. Now that you have cleared your mind and relaxed your body, think of something to make you happy and smile as you do it. It doesn't matter what it is as long as it amuses *you*, as all you are trying to do here is to make yourself feel happy. This

is a basic visualisation exercise and it really does work,. It is very hard to feel unhappy if you have a smile on your face anyway, but if you are thinking of something funny at the same time it is nearly impossible. If you are sceptical try it now and you will be pleasantly surprised.

4. Lastly, run through the opening lines of your speech in your mind so that when you stand up you will not have to concentrate on what you are going to say. If you have learnt your whole speech off by heart this should be no problem, but even if you are using prompt cards you should, as a minimum, make sure that you have learnt the opening few lines of it by heart to the extent that you can recite them at the drop of a hat.

SAMPLE SPEECH TWELVE

A reasonably short speech, with wittily ironic references to the young bridesmaids, this speech is pithy and relaxed. It helps that this best man is married himself, so he can probably remember exactly what it was like to be in the groom's shoes. He has produced a sympathetic, and amusing speech which is delivered with elan.

Hullo, and for those of you that have no idea who I am, my name is Steven and I'm Mike's Best Man. I am very friendly, housebroken, I seldom bite and in the near future, can probably be found near the bar, so if any of you want to know more details than those that I am about to share in my speech, please feel free to ask.

First, I want to start by offering thanks to the bridesmaids. You did an amazing job with all you had to do – I mean clutching a bouquet of flowers, looking pretty, and trying to hold that little pout-like look is not something that is easy to achieve. Even so, you each did a splendid job and you look amazingly beautiful. I also want to point out that Sara is stunning – the most beautiful bride I've ever laid eyes on . . . except for you sweetness, of course [turns to address wife].

Ideally, you want to have an open posture, so stand with your legs slightly apart, roughly the width of your body, and with one foot a little in front of the other. Put most of your weight on your front foot and extend your arms slightly out to your side. If you are using notes hold them in one hand and only raise them every now and then as a prompt. Do not lift your notes to eye-level to read them as this will hide your face from the audience and create a barrier; try not to raise your notes any higher than chest level and simply glance down at them.

Eye contact: Another way to ensure that the audience feels involved in your speech is to maintain eye contact with them. Obviously, you will not be able to look at everyone in the audience all the time, but you can sweep your eyes across the room as you speak. The most effective way to do this is to slowly follow an imaginary Z shape across the room with your eyes. When you get to the top or bottom of the Z go back the other way and change the size of the Z each time you do this so that you cover the whole of the audience during the course of the speech. If you are mentioning anyone in the audience by name in your speech look at them and smile when you do so (it is also a good idea to gesture in their direction at the same time as this will show other people where they are as you mention them).

Tone of voice: Even at the most formal weddings, the best man's speech is expected to be light and amusing with a little sentiment. This should be reflected in the tone of voice you use to make your speech. It is quite likely that you will have a number of friends in the audience – imagine that you are speaking to them as you make your speech. Keep your tone friendly and conversational throughout. If the final draft of your speech has been written in a conversational style to suit you, this should come quite naturally and will make reading the speech easier. The tone of voice you use will greatly influence how your speech is received, so speak with energy and conviction to achieve the best presentation of your speech.

Be audible: No matter how good your speech is, or how well you present it, if it can't be heard or understood then all your effort will have gone to waste. The golden rules here are to speak slowly and clearly. While you should be trying to maintain a conversational tone you will need to speak a little more slowly than you would in normal conversation. If there is a microphone available then you would be well advised to use it, as this should ensure that you are heard by one and all (ideally you should hold a microphone eight to ten inches from your mouth if you do have the opportunity to use one). If there is not a microphone available then be sure to speak loudly enough so that the people furthest away can also hear you.

SAMPLE SPEECH THIRTEEN

A simple and joyful speech by an old friend of the groom, this combines self-deprecating jokes, a couple of anecdotes at the groom's expense, and genuine pleasure at the happy couple's marriage.

Good evening family and friends. Thank you for joining Mike and Sara on their wedding day. First, on behalf of the bride and groom, I want to thank the bridesmaids. You added a magical touch to this wedding. Additionally, I want to extend a note of gratitude to the Maid of Honour, the groomsmen, the flower girl and ring bearer, the ushers, and reader – you all played a very important role today. Because of your hard work and devotion, this was an incredibly beautiful wedding.

For those that don't know who I am, my name is Richard and I'm Mike's Best Man. I specifically remember the day Mike asked if I would stand up with him as Best Man and thinking to myself – why me?. I kept thinking, why didn't he ask someone more qualified, someone with a great sense of humour, someone that could easily memorise the speech…(looking at cue cards) … I'm sorry, where was I …

Here we go – think about the human brain and what a wonderful thing it isn't – the damn thing never stops

191

working. From the minute that you're born until the day that you get ready to write the Best Man speech, your brain works just fine and then for some reason, it stops!

Anyway, I want to tell you what a great friend Mike has been to me. Through thick and thin, good and bad, he's always stood by me with amazing strength and faithfulness. For example, I especially remember him being there on that truly awful day when I trashed my brand new car – oh wait, Mike was driving.

It was a horrible accident. He was trying to show off in my car, speeding along until we came to a place in the road with a sharp curve. Mike slammed on the brakes, except he pressed on that other pedal, the accelerator.

The car shot across the road, barely missed a brick wall, hit an embankment, and then flew into the air. When we finally came to a stop, we were sitting in a tree with all four wheels dangling in the air. I have to give Mike some credit though … he did try to put the car in reverse to set us free!

Growing up, Mike was known around the neighbourhood for several things. First, he was known as the "kid with the Dumbo elephant ears", then he was known for being a very poor dresser, and third, he had the reputation of riding his unicycle everywhere he went, somehow thinking that made him look cool. I don't get it. How could someone like that land such a catch, the beautiful, intelligent, and witty woman that is Sara?

In all seriousness, I have never been more proud of anyone in my life. Mike I'm so excited and happy that you met the most amazing woman who you can now call your wife. I am convinced that you two will survive whatever googlies life throws your way.

I would like to ask everyone to stand and join me in a toast to the bride and groom, as they continue the celebration as husband and wife! To my dearest friends – Mike and Sara Johnson – keep things in your marriage exciting and always enjoy the unexpected!

SAMPLE SPEECH FOURTEEN

The best man, the groom's youngest brother, seems a little overwhelmed by the job of best man and this speech does not flow as easily as some of the others. However, it ends with an especially warm, earnest and heartfelt tribute to the groom and his new bride.

For guests that don't know who I am, my name is John and I'm not only Mike's Best Man but also his youngest brother. I want to begin by thanking everyone for coming today to celebrate the union of Mike and Sara!

I also want to say a little about the role of being the Best Man at a wedding. Personally, I believe the title is a little overboard. After all, if I'm the "best man", then why is Sara with Mike? Therefore, I think a more appropriate title for me in this role would be to be Mike's Good Man, leaving the title of "best man" to Mike.

What I've discovered is that being the Best Man is an awesome role. At first, I thought this would be a breeze, but I soon learned that I shouldn't take it so lightly. To make sure I didn't forget anything, I conducted a great deal of research so that nothing was overlooked. What I discovered was that I now had a huge checklist of responsibilities associated with being Best Man. [Pull out an extremely long piece of paper to represent the checklist.]

First, Mike was born in December of 1975. He was actually a premature baby, weighing in at just five pounds. Our mother thought him being born early had something to do with his backward thinking. For instance, I remember once Mum took Mike to the doctor when he was very young because he kept getting sick. Speaking with authority, Mike told the doctor he knew what the problem was. When the doctor asked him for his opinion, Mike confidently blurted out, "I'm pregnant!"

Even though Mike was born outside of the disco era, he loved the music long after it was fashionable. Out dancing one night in his John Travolta suit, he saw a beautiful woman across the dance floor, and that was Sara. As I understand it, and Sara you may need to correct me later, you were the one that made the first move in getting to know Mike. I guess after dancing the night away, the pair headed out for breakfast and have been inseparable every since, although I hope they're both avoiding the discos.

For those of you looking at Sara and then Mike, only to ask yourself, "why?" just remember that love is blind! In all honesty, I'm thrilled that the two of you found each other and

I hope that neither of you will never, ever, need my services as Best Man again!

While most of Mike and Sara's close friends and family members were able to make it to the wedding tonight, there were some people that couldn't be here. However, we did receive a few messages from those people, and there is one in particular that I wanted to read.

From David (Mike's close friend) – *I want to wish you and Sara all the best. You know that they say a successful marriage is a 50/50 partnership, but I do hope you realise that people who believe that actually don't know anything when it comes to either women or fractions! Sorry Sara…*

On behalf of the bride and groom, I want to thank everyone here for sharing in this special day, particularly those of you that have travelled long distances. I started planning my speech about six months ago and after hearing it, you probably think it feels like it took six months to give.

Regardless, it gives me immense pleasure (and relief) to invite all of you to stand, raise your glasses, and join me in toasting the new, Mr and Mrs Mike Johnson. While we're all still standing, I would like to say a few things – Mike, you've been my best friend and a terrific brother. Being here with you today is a real honour. You've taught me so much while we were growing up, and if I can be half the man, you are and marry a woman half as beautiful and wonderful as Sara, then I will have succeeded in life. I can honestly say that today I'm almost jealous of you, and as your friend and younger brother, I wish you and Sara all the happiness in the world.

Practice makes perfect

Now that you know what you are going to say and how to say it, you need to practise until you are completely comfortable with your speech. A great way to do this is in three stages.

1. Learn your lines. Initially, you just need to get to grips with learning your speech. Ideally you will be able to memorise the whole speech – and this is one of the advantages of keeping it short. If you are unable to do this, you should at least try to learn your opening lines and closing lines off by heart. This will ensure that you are able to look at the audience when you first address them and when you come to propose a toast at the end of your speech. The best way to learn your speech is to sit down on your own and read it through to yourself. Don't worry too much at this stage about how it sounds: your main concern is to remember what you are going to say. As you have spent considerable effort writing and refining your speech you will probably be very familiar with it and you should find this quite easy. Once you are confident that you are able to read your speech with minimal reference to your prompt cards, you are ready to begin practising the delivery of the speech.

2. Delivery. It's now time to start putting some of the skills that
    were discussed in the previous section into practice . There
    are two ways in which you can really get to grips with how
    best to present your speech: standing in front of a full-length
    mirror, and audio taping yourself as you do so. (Alternatively,
    if you have a video camera you could film yourself and kill
    two birds with one stone). By standing in front of a mirror
    while reading your speech you can begin to work on your
    visual presentation. It is a good idea to start by sitting in a
    chair in front of the mirror as this accurately reflects the
    situation you will be in when you finally come to give your
    speech at the wedding. Begin by going through the relaxation
    exercises discussed earlier and then stand up and start to
    present your speech. By this stage, you should know what you
    are going to say and it's time to start working on how you are
    going to put it across to the audience, hence the emphasis on
    presenting, rather than just reading, your speech.

    The first things to look out for are any distracting
    movements or gestures which you may have. Most people do
    all sorts of things unconsciously while they are talking, such
    as shuffling their feet, stroking their chin or fiddling with the
    change in their pocket. If you notice that you are doing
    anything like this, you must consciously stop yourself as it will

distract an audience from what you are saying. If you practise for long enough and make yourself speak without doing these things it will become second nature to you. Once you have eliminated any distracting movements, start to get used to the open stance you want to assume while you are giving your speech and also begin to put some real emotion into what you are saying. Keep working on your presentation until you are completely happy with it and can run through your speech without hesitation.

3. Practise with an audience. Once you have perfected the presentation of your speech it is time to practise in front of an audience. Obviously you will not be able to get a crowd of people as large as that at the reception to practise on, but it is great preparation to rehearse in front of two or three people just so that you are used to giving your speech to an audience. Friends or colleagues at work are the ideal people to ask for this. The kind of people you should choose are those who you can trust to give you honest feedback from the experience. Once you have a couple of volunteers, run through your speech from start to finish using all the delivery skills you have learned and practised. Don't be surprised or concerned if you fluff your lines or feel embarrassed the first

couple of times you do it, as it is perfectly natural to do so. This is why it is a good idea to practise with a small audience whose opinions you can trust. Once you are happy with the performance of your speech, ask your test audience for some positive feedback. Make sure that they are aware that you are not looking to make wholesale changes to either the speech or your delivery, but simply to fine-tune any areas that may need a slight improvement.

Ideally, you should try to have the speech written and all your practising done at least a week before the wedding. This means that you won't have to worry about your speech during the busy build-up to the big day. If you manage to do this then you should just run through your speech a couple of times each night to keep it fresh in your mind.

You have now done all you can to ensure that your speech will be a memorable one, both for you and the audience at the reception, so there is only one last piece of advice to give: relax and enjoy the experience.

SAMPLE SPEECH FIFTEEN

This speech avoids any personal anecdotes about the groom's youthful exploits and sticks to lighter jokes without attempting any character assasination. This gives the speech a slightly impersonal flavour, but, it is well constructed, short and the best man is obviously sincere in his good wishes for the bride and groom.

Good afternoon family and friends. My name is Jeff and today, I have the honour of being Mike's Best Man. First, on behalf of the wedding party, I would like to thank each of you for making this wedding a wonderful and memorable occasion. Each one of you put in tremendous time and effort and as everyone can see, you did a fantastic job!

For all of the guests who travelled long distances or even from abroad to join Mike and Sara on this special day – I find it amazing just how far people will go to get a free meal! No, seriously, your presence is much appreciated and the wedding would not have been the same without you here!

When Mike asked me if I would be his Best Man, I said yes and then immediately stopped by the nearest library to learn everything I could about my role. One of the things I read in a number of books was that I had to maintain a clear head throughout the wedding and reception – that's when I got up and walked out! All the way home, I kept saying to myself, "What was Mike thinking?"

While conducting my research, I did come across some very useful information. For example, I discovered that a wedding consisted of three primary elements. The Aisle – the longest distance the groom will ever travel. The Altar – the place where the groom's life is forever changed. The Hymn – a celebration of the marriage.

The reason that I mentioned this is that as I was milling about before the wedding today, I realised that Sara, bless her heart, had read the same information. Everywhere she went I could hear her whispering under her breath, "Aisle, Altar, Hymn – Aisle, Altar, Hymn – Aisle, Altar, Hymn".

As the Best Man, I have a huge laundry list of responsibilities. For example, I was supposed to make sure that Mike showed up to the wedding on time, that he was sober, dressed appropriately, and so on. Looking at him now, I guess I didn't do such a bad job considering the canvas with which I had to work.

I had to restrain from sniggering during the wedding ceremony when the minister make the statement "For better or worse". I kept thinking that Mike couldn't have done any better and Sara couldn't have done any worse.

No, not really! The two of them truly make the perfect couple. With all honesty and sincerity, Mike, I want to thank you for entrusting the role of Best Man to me. It has been a privilege to stand beside you, as you exchanged wedding vows with Sara, and now embark on a new life with your beautiful wife.

If I could please ask everyone here today to stand with me and raise your glasses, let's offer a toast to the newly married Mike and Sara Johnson. Our wish for you is that life is filled with all good things.

SAMPLE SPEECH SIXTEEN

After thanking the wedding party for all their hard work, the best man reveals the shared history of a lifetime of friendship with the groom with a selection of funny and affectionate anecdotes. This is a very genuine speech, in spite of the traditional jokes at the groom's expense.

I would like to thank each of you for joining Mike and Sara on this very special day. I would also like to tell each member of the wedding party what a wonderful job they did today in making this an occasion to remember. My name is Kevin and as Mike's Best Man, I feel very privileged. What can I say about Mike – I've known him for more than 18 years. Mike is intelligent, handsome, charismatic, witty . . .oh sorry, I'm at the wrong wedding!

When Mike and I met, we were both at primary school. To be honest, neither one of us was what you would call thin or in shape. Our mothers, being the kind women that they are, would simply encourage us by telling us that we were merely "big boned". The truth is – we were fat! In fact, the first time I met Mike he was standing on the corner of Tom Road … and Dick Street … and Harry Crescent! However, with lots of patience, encouragement from each other and sheer determination, you can now see what svelte studs we have both become.

Without doubt, Mike is an interesting character. He has had a long-held passion for football, often doing whatever it took to get great tickets. I can even remember one time when he was promised excellent seats if he would dress up as a woman and then walk into the local McDonald's to order food to go. Without hesitating, Mike donned his sister's dress, borrowed a wig and make-up, and off he went to get a Big Mac. Now I don't know about you, but I think I would rather just pay the price of the ticket.

Out of boredom in 1998, Mike and I got this excellent idea that we could pass the time by going out to test drive cars. Now remember that we were not just any old geezers, but two studs.

Heading to the local BMW dealership, we laid eyes on a black 7-series and decided that was the car to drive. Trying to impress me with his manly driving skills, Mike took the car out onto the motorway where he opened it up. Beaming with pride, Mike turned to me and said, "Look there Kevin, we're cruising at 115 miles per hour". Of course, I had to point out to him that he was looking at the clock and not the speedometer, meaning it was 1:15 p.m.!

Mike has always been a great friend, one that can make anyone laugh. Through the years of knowing Mike and being his closest friend, I have grown to respect and love him just like a brother. What I know is that when Mike met Sara, his entire world changed – all for the better.

Never in my life have I seen two people more made for each other. I would like to ask everyone here tonight to stand with me and offer a toast to Mike and Sara Johnson as they begin new life together. In addition to wishing you both lots of love and happiness, we all wish you years of adventure and excitement! Many, many congratulations to you both on your marriage.

SAMPLE SPEECH SEVENTEEN

This speech is performed by an old friend of the groom who uses old college anecdotes to illustrate the finer points of the groom's character. The best man emphasises his long-standing relationship with the groom and there is the merest hint that he does not know the bride too well.

I would like to begin by thanking everyone for celebrating with Mike and Sara on this very special day. To begin, my name is Sam and as Mike's best friend of 20 years, I've been asked to stand up as his Best Man. I was just handed a note by the building management that for health and safety reasons, you will need to stay off the tabletops and chairs while giving me a standing ovation.

I think everyone here agrees that this was a beautiful wedding. Unfortunately, the downside is that you now have to listen to me speak for a few minutes.

I want to start by thanking the entire wedding party on behalf of the bride and groom for all the hard work that has made this such a magical day. Mike, I personally want to thank you for the opportunity you've given me today and especially for finally admitting, after all these years, that I am in fact the "best man".

I have to admit that I've been very nervous about this, but Mike has been great in offering me lots of encouragement. I want to share a little bit about Mike, starting when we were in college. He was the only guy I knew that had a pool table in the living room and a miniature fridge in the bathroom. There was, of course, a lock on the fridge, and the pool table took two-pound coins. Mike only charged a small deposit for the loan of a cue, though it was slightly more if you wanted one with a tip on the end. Although I have to say, everyone loved spending time at this unconventional pad.

Most of us in college assumed that Mike would stay a bachelor for a long time. Part of this was because he claimed he would be the last man standing and the other part was that we simply couldn't imagine anyone wanting to accept his unique style of decorating. Therefore, when Mike told me he had met a wonderful woman, fallen in love, and asked her to marry him I was surprised. Although I love Mike like a brother, I had to ask myself what this woman could possibly see in him. But of course, as the old saying goes, love is blind and marriage is a real eye-opener!

While I was trying to figure out what to say in my speech, I learned that when Sara was a little girl, her favourite toy was a colourful clown doll. That's when it hit me how funny it is that history has a tendency of repeating itself. Just 26 years ago, Sara's family was tucking her in at night with a stuffed clown and well, here we are again today!

I'll never forget the time when Mike and Sara were dating and he came up with the idea of cleaning her dirty fish tank as a way of surprising her. Leaving the fish in the tank while about 90% of the water was drained, Mike quickly wiped down the sides of the tank to remove any algae. Feeling very proud of himself, he retired to the living room to wait for Sara so he could show her the good deed.

After walking in the door, Mike eagerly guided her to the room with the fish tank when they both gasped in horror. What Mike hadn't realised is that the sponge he used to clean the inside of the tank had built-in soap … Needless to say, the tank was overflowing with bubbles and the fish – well, Mike made a special trip to the pet shop the following morning!

Even though Mike is not perfect, he is a great guy and I'm very happy for him and Sara. Mike, my friend, it's been a real pleasure in acting as your Best Man, but more importantly, knowing that you have been my friend for so many years and will continue to be so.

As everyone stands to raise their glasses with me, it gives me immense joy, not to mention complete relief, to congratulate you on your marriage and wish you a life full of fun and happiness. Ladies and gentlemen, I would like to introduce to you, Mr and Mrs Mike Johnson.

A Miscellany of Toasts and Quotations

Toasts

* May you both live as long as you want,
  And never want as long as you live.

* May you be poor in misfortune,
  Rich in blessings,
  Slow to make enemies,
  And quick to make friends.
  But rich or poor, quick or slow,
  May you know nothing but happiness
  From this day forward.

* As you slide down the bannister of life,
  May the splinters never point the wrong way.

* May the joys of today
  Be those of tomorrow.
  The goblets of life
  Hold no dregs of sorrow.

* May the saddest day of your future be no worse
  Than the happiest day of your past.

* May the most you wish for
  Be the least you get.

* May your troubles be less
  And your blessings be more.
  And nothing but happiness
  Come through your door.

* May brooks and trees and singing hills
  Join in the chorus, too.
  And every gentle wind that blows
  Send happiness to you.

* May the roof above you never fall in.
  And may the friends gathered below it never fall out.

* May you have warm words on a cold evening,
  A full moon on a dark night,
  And the road downhill all the way to your door.

* May there be a generation of children
  From the children of your children.

* Here's to health and prosperity,
  To you and all your posterity.
  And them that doesn't drink with sincerity,
  That they may be damned for all eternity!

* May you see each other through many dark days,
  and make all the rest a little brighter.
* May all your ups and downs come only in the bedroom.
* My greatest wish for the two of you is that through the years your
  love for each other will so deepen and grow, that years from now
  you will look back on this day, your wedding day, as the day you
  loved each other the least.
* It don't matter where you get your appetite, as long as you eat at
  home!
* May the best day of your past be the worst day of your future.
* May the roof above you never fall in and may you both never fall
  out.
* To the lamp of love – may it burn brightest in the darkest hours and
  never flicker in the winds of trial.
* May 'for better or worse' be far better than worse.
* The man or woman you really love will never grow old to you.
  Through the wrinkles of time, through the bowed frame of years,
  You will always see the dear face and feel the warm heart union of
  your eternal love.
* May you have many children and may they grow mature in taste
  and healthy in colour and as sought-after as the contents of the
  glass.
* Let us toast the health of the bride; Let us toast the health of the

groom, Let us toast the person that tied; Let us toast every guest in the room.

* Remember that if you ever put your marital problems on the back burner they are sure to boil over.
* Happy marriages begin when we marry the one we love, and they blossom when we love the one we married.

Quotations

Love:

Love takes off masks that we fear we cannot live without and know we cannot live within.
JAMES BALDWIN (1924–87)

Love is the immortal flow of energy that nourishes, extends and preserves. Its eternal goal is life.
SMILEY BLANTON

We perceive when love begins and when it declines by our embarrassment when alone together.
LA BRUYERE (1645–1696)

The best proof of love is trust.
JOYCE BROTHERS

Sometimes the heart sees what is invisible to the eye.
H. JACKSON BROWN JR.

Perfect love is rare indeed – for to be a lover will require that you continually have the subtlety of the very wise, the flexibility of the child, the sensitivity of the artist, the understanding of the philosopher, the acceptance of the saint, the tolerance of the scholar and the fortitude of the certain.
LEO BUSCAGLIA

Where there is great love, there are always wishes.
WILLA CATHER

A relationship is like a rose, How long it lasts, no one knows; Love can erase an awful past, Love can be yours, you'll see at last; To feel that love, it makes you sigh, To have it leave, you'd rather die; You hope you've found that special rose, 'Cause you love and care for the one you chose.
ROB CELLA

Love builds bridges where there are none.
R. H. DELANEY

Sympathy constitutes friendship; but in love there is a sort of antipathy, or opposing passion. Each strives to be the other, and both together make up one whole.
SAMUEL TAYLOR COLERIDGE (1772–1834)

All thoughts, all passions, all delights Whatever stirs this mortal frame All are but ministers of Love And feed His sacred flame.
SAMUEL TAYLOR COLERIDGE (1772–1834)

Woe to the man whose heart has not learned while young to hope, to love – and to put its trust in life.
JOSEPH CONRAD (1857–1924)

Absence is to love what wind is to fire; it extinguishes the small, it enkindles the great.
COMTE DEBUSSY-RABUTIN

We are all born for love. It is the principle of existence, and its only end.
BENJAMIN DISRAELI (1804–1881)

The art of love ... is largely the art of persistence.
ALBERT ELLIS

Come live with me, and be my love, And we will some new pleasures prove Of golden sands, and crystal brooks, With silken lines, and silver hooks.
JOHN DONNE (1572–1631), *The Bait*

You will find as you look back upon your life that the moments when you have truly lived are the moments when you have done things in the spirit of love.
HENRY DRUMMOND (1851–1897)

All mankind love a lover.
RALPH WALDO EMERSON (1803–1882)

The hardest of all is learning to be a well of affection, and not a fountain; to show them we love them not when we feel like it, but when they do.
NAN FAIRBROTHER

There is only one terminal dignity – love.
HELEN HAYES

Immature love says: 'I love you because I need you.' Mature love says 'I need you because I love you.'
ERICH FROMM (1900–1980)

In love the paradox occurs that two beings become one and yet remain two.
ERICH FROMM (1900–1980)

Where there is love there is life.
MAHATMA GANDHI (1869–1948)

For it was not into my ear you whispered, but into my heart. It was not my lips you kissed, but my soul.
JUDY GARLAND (1922–1969)

Life without love is like a tree without blossoms or fruit.
KAHLIL GIBRAN, *The Vision*

Looking back, I have this to regret, that too often when I loved, I did not say so.
DAVID GRAYSON

The supreme happiness in life is the conviction that we are loved —
loved for ourselves, or rather, loved in spite of ourselves.
VICTOR HUGO (1802–1885)

The moment you have in your heart this extraordinary thing called
love and feel the depth, the delight, the ecstasy of it, you will discover
that for you the world is transformed.
J. KRISHNAMURTI (1895–1986)

Being deeply loved by someone gives you strength; loving someone
deeply gives you courage.
LAO-TZU (6th century BC)

There is no disguise which can hide love for long where it exists, or
simulate it where it does not.
LA ROCHEFOUCAULD (1613–1680)

Treasure the love you receive above all. It will survive long after your
good health has vanished.
OG MANDINO

Do all things with love.
OG MANDINO

The only abnormality is the incapacity to love.
ANAÏS NIN (1903–77)

At the touch of love everyone becomes a poet.
PLATO (*c.*428–348 BC)

We all suffer from the preoccupation that there exists ... in the loved
one, perfection.
SIDNEY POITIER (1924–)

The cure for all ills and wrongs, the cares, the sorrows and the crimes
of humanity, all lie in the one word 'love.' It is the divine vitality that
everywhere produces and restores life.
LYDIA MARIA CHILD

To fear love is to fear life, and those who fear life are already three
parts dead.
BERTRAND RUSSELL (1872–1970)

Tell me who admires you and loves you, and I will tell you who
you are.
CHARLES AUGUSTIN SAINTE-BEAUVE (1804–1869)

I have said nothing because there is nothing I can say that would describe how I feel as perfectly as you deserve it.

KYLE SCHMIDT

Love means never having to say you're sorry.

ERICH SEGAL

Romeo, Romeo, wherefore art thou, Romeo? / Deny thy father, and refuse thy name...

WILLIAM SHAKESPEARE (1564–1623)

To fall in love is easy, even to remain in it is not difficult; our human loneliness is cause enough. But it is a hard quest worth making to find a comrade through whose steady presence one becomes steadily the person one desires to be.

ANNA LOUISE STRONG

If you judge people, you have no time to love them.

MOTHER THERESA (1910–1997)

You don't love a woman because she is beautiful, but she is beautiful because you love her.

ANON

If you love somebody, let them go. If they return, they were always yours. If they don't, they never were.

ANON

Love has nothing to do with what you are expecting to get, it's what you are expected to give — which is everything.

ANON

Love does not begin and end the way we seem to think it does. Love is a battle, love is a war; love is a growing up.

JAMES BALDWIN (1924-1987)

Never pretend to a love which you do not actually feel, for love is not ours to command.

ALAN WATTS

To love deeply in one direction makes us more loving in all others.

ANNE-SOPHIE SWETCHINE

Perhaps the feelings that we experience when we are in love represent a normal state. Being in love shows a person who he should be.

ANTON CHEKHOV (1860–1904)

Love is not enough. It must be the foundation, the cornerstone – but not the complete structure. It is much too pliable, too yielding.
BETTE DAVIS (1908–1989)

Clarity of mind means clarity of passion, too; this is why a great and clear mind loves ardently and sees distinctly what it loves.
BLAISE PASCAL (1623–1662)

The meeting of two personalities is like the contact of two chemical substances: if there is any reaction, both are transformed.
CARL JUNG (1875–1961)

Nothing takes the taste out of peanut butter quite like unrequited love.
CHARLES M. SCHULZ (1922–2000), Charlie Brown in *Peanuts*

To love and be loved is to feel the sun from both sides.
DAVID VISCOTT, *O* Magazine, February 2004

There's a lot to be said for self-delusionment when it comes to matters of the heart.
DIANE FROLOV AND ANDREW SCHNEIDER, *Northern Exposure*, 1993

Oh, life is a glorious cycle of song,

A medley of extemporanea;

And love is a thing that can never go wrong;

And I am Marie of Romania.

DOROTHY PARKER (1893–1967), *Not So Deep as a Well*

All love that has not friendship for its base, is like a mansion built upon sand.

ELLA WHEELER WILCOX, *O* Magazine, February 2004

Love is everything it's cracked up to be…It really is worth fighting for, being brave for, risking everything for.

ERICA JONG, *O* Magazine, February 2004

When love is in excess it brings a man nor honour nor any worthiness.

EURIPIDES (484–406 BC), *Medea*

Love is the triumph of imagination over intelligence.

H. L. MENCKEN (1880–1956)

There is always some madness in love. But there is also always some reason in madness.

FRIEDRICH NIETZSCHE (1844–1900), *On Reading and Writing*

What else is love but understanding and rejoicing in the fact that another person lives, acts, and experiences otherwise than we do …?
FRIEDRICH NIETZSCHE (1844–1900)

I cannot think well of a man who sports with any woman's feelings; and there may often be a great deal more suffered than a stander-by can judge of.
JANE AUSTEN (1775–1817), *Mansfield Park*

Sometimes when you look back on a situation, you realize it wasn't all you thought it was. A beautiful girl walked into your life. You fell in love. Or did you? Maybe it was only a childish infatuation, or maybe just a brief moment of vanity.
HENRY BROMEL, *Northern Exposure*, The Big Kiss, 1991

There is no remedy for love but to love more.
HENRY DAVID THOREAU (1817–1862), *Journal*

Just because you love someone doesn't mean you have to be involved with them. Love is not a bandage to cover wounds.
HUGH ELLIOTT, *Standing Room Only* weblog, February 2004

Passion makes the world go round. Love just makes it a safer place.
ICE T, *The Ice Opinion*

But when a young lady is to be a heroine, the perverseness of forty
surrounding families cannot prevent her. Something must and will
happen to throw a hero in her way.
JANE AUSTEN (1775–1817), *Northanger Abbey*

Love is the difficult realization that something other than
oneself is real.
IRIS MURDOCH (1919–1999)

We can only learn to love by loving.
IRIS MURDOCH (1919–1999)

The enthusiasm of a woman's love is even beyond the biographer's.
JANE AUSTEN (1775–1817), *Mansfield Park*

Love is, above all else, the gift of oneself.
JEAN ANOUILH (1910–1987)

Age does not protect you from love. But love, to some extent, protects you from age.
JEANNE MOREAU (1928–)

'Tis the most tender part of love, each other to forgive.
JOHN SHEFFIELD (1648–1721)

Is love supposed to last throughout all time, or is it like trains changing at random stops. If I loved her, how could I leave her? If I felt that way then, how come I don't feel anything now?
JEFF MELVOIN, *Northern Exposure*, Altered Egos, 1993

True love brings up everything - you're allowing a mirror to be held up to you daily.
JENNIFER ANISTON, *O* Magazine, February 2004

Love is the delightful interval between meeting a beautiful girl and discovering that she looks like a haddock.
JOHN BARRYMORE (1882–1942)

Love is an act of endless forgiveness, a tender look which becomes a habit.
PETER USTINOV (1921–2004)

Gravity. It keeps you rooted to the ground. In space, there's not any gravity. You just kind of leave your feet and go floating around. Is that what being in love is like?

JOSH BRAND AND JOHN FALSEY, *Northern Exposure*, The Pilot, 1990

How we treasure (and admire) the people who acknowledge us!

JULIE MORGENSTERN, *O* Magazine, Belatedly Yours, January 2004

To love is to receive a glimpse of heaven.

KAREN SUNDE

Honesty is the only way with anyone, when you'll be so close as to be living inside each other's skins.

LOIS MCMASTER BUJOLD, *A Civil Campaign*, 1999

When you give each other everything, it becomes an even trade. Each wins all.

LOIS MCMASTER BUJOLD, *A Civil Campaign*, 1999

Love is an exploding cigar we willingly smoke.

LYNDA BARRY

Real love is a permanently self-enlarging experience.
M. SCOTT PECK, *O* Magazine, February 2004

To be brave is to love someone unconditionally, without expecting anything in return. To just give. That takes courage, because we don't want to fall on our faces or leave ourselves open to hurt.
MADONNA (1958–), *O* Magazine, January 2004

Love is the big booming beat which covers up the noise of hate.
MARGARET CHO, weblog, January 2004

Think about a woman. Doesn't know you're thinking about her. Doesn't care you're thinking about her. Makes you think about her even more.
MARTIN SAGE AND SYBIL ADELMAN, *Northern Exposure*, The Bumpy Road to Love, 1991

Love is a snowmobile racing across the tundra and then suddenly it flips over, pinning you underneath. At night, the ice weasels come.
MATT GROENING (1954–), *Life in Hell*

Learning to love yourself is the greatest love of all.
MICHAEL MASSER AND LINDA CREED

Fall not in love, therefore; it will stick to your face.
NATIONAL LAMPOON, "Deteriorata"

The first duty of love is to listen.
PAUL TILLICH (1886–1965), *O* Magazine, February 2004

Love is not blind – it sees more, not less. But because it sees
more, it is willing to see less.
RABBI JULIUS GORDON

For one human being to love another; that is perhaps the most
difficult of all our tasks, the ultimate, the last test and proof, the work
for which all other work is but preparation.
RAINER MARIA RILKE (1875–1926)

He who is in love is wise and is becoming wiser, sees newly every time
he looks at the object beloved, drawing from it with his eyes and his
mind those virtues which it possesses.
RALPH WALDO EMERSON (1803–1882), Address on *The Method of Nature*

I believe love is primarily a choice and only sometimes a feeling. If
you want to feel love, choose to love and be patient.
REAL LIVE PREACHER, RealLivePreacher.com Weblog, December 2002

I don't think anyone can DO anything that would make him worthy of love. Love is a gift and cannot be earned. It can only be given.
REAL LIVE PREACHER, RealLivePreacher.com Weblog, January 2003

You can't love anyone until you understand that you can't love everyone.
REAL LIVE PREACHER, RealLivePreacher.com Weblog, October 2003

Before I met my husband, I'd never fallen in love, though I'd stepped in it a few times.
RITA RUDNER

Love is an irresistible desire to be irresistibly desired.
ROBERT FROST (1874–1963)

One word frees us of all the weight and pain of life: That word is love.
SOPHOCLES (496–406 BC)

Love is or it ain't. Thin love ain't love at all.
TONI MORRISON (1931–), *Beloved*

Never marry but for love; but see that thou lovest what is lovely.
WILLIAM PENN (1644–1718)

Love isn't a decision. It's a feeling. If we could decide who we loved, it would be much simplier, but much less magical.
TREY PARKER AND MATT STONE, *South Park*

Life's greatest happiness is to be convinced we are loved.
VICTOR HUGO (1802–1885), *Les Miserables*

A woman can forgive a man for the harm he does her ... but she can never forgive him for the sacrifices he makes on her account.
W. SOMERSET MAUGHAM (1874–1965), *The Moon and Sixpence*

The important thing was to love rather than to be loved.
W. SOMERSET MAUGHAM (1874–1965), *Of Human Bondage*

There's always one who loves and one who lets himself be loved.
W. SOMERSET MAUGHAM (1874–1965), *Of Human Bondage*

The hours I spend with you I look upon as sort of a perfumed garden, a dim twilight, and a fountain singing to it … you and you alone make me feel that I am alive … Other men it is said have seen angels, but I have seen thee and thou art enough.
GEORGE MOORE (1852–1933)

There's only one thing greater than my fear – that is my love. My love will always conquer my fear – but it can't do it immediately. It needs the full force of my love to do it and it takes days for that to emerge out of its dark hiding places.

JOHN MIDDLETON MURRY (1889–1957)

I cannot exist without you – I am forgetful of every thing but seeing you again – my Life seems to stop there – I see no further. You have absorb'd me. I have a sensation at the present moment as though I were dissolving … I have been astonished that Men could die Martyrs for religion – I have shudder'd at it – I shudder no more – I could be martyr'd for my Religion – Love is my religion – I could die for that – I could die for you. My creed is Love and you are its only tenet – You have ravish'd me away by a Power I cannot resist.

JOHN KEATS (1795–1821)

A man falls in love through his eyes, a woman through her ears.

WOODROW WYATT (1918–1997)

How on earth are you ever going to explain in terms of chemistry and physics so important a biological phenomenon as first love?

ALBERT EINSTEIN (1870–1955)

In our life there is a single color, as on an artist's palette, which provides the meaning of life and art. It is the color of love.
MARC CHAGALL (1887–1985)

Love is an ideal thing, marriage a real thing; a confusion of the real with the ideal never goes unpunished.
JOHANN WOLFGANG VON GOETHE (1749–1832)

Life is short and we have never too much time for gladdening the hearts of those who are travelling the dark journey with us. Oh be swift to love, make haste to be kind.
HENRI FREDERIC AMIEL (1821–1881)

In love, as in war, a fortress that parleys is half taken.
MARGARET OF VALOIS (1553–1615)

Friendship:

When I find myself fading, I close my eyes and realise my friends are my energy.
ANON

The road to a friend's house is never long.
DANISH PROVERB

Friendship is the hardest thing in the world to explain. It's not something you learn in school. But if you haven't learned the meaning of friendship, you really haven't learned anything.
MUHAMMAD ALI (1942–)

Don't walk behind me, I may not lead. Don't walk in front of me, I may not follow. Just walk beside me and be my friend.
ALBERT CAMUS (1913–1960)

The only way to have a friend is to be one.
RALPH WALDO EMERSON (1803–1882)

Friends are treasures.
HORACE BRUNS

A friendship can weather most things and thrive in thin soil; but it needs a little mulch of letters and phone calls and small, silly presents every so often – just to save it from drying out completely.
PAM BROWN

The real test of friendship is: can you literally do nothing with the other person? Can you enjoy those moments of life that are utterly simple?
EUGENE KENNEDY

We call that person who has lost his father, an orphan; and a widower that man who has lost his wife. But that man who has known the immense unhappiness of losing a friend, by what name do we call him? Here every language is silent and holds its peace in impotence.
JOSEPH ROUX

True friends stab you in the front.
OSCAR WILDE (1854–1900)

You can make more friends in two months by becoming interested in other people than you can in two years by trying to get other people interested in you.
DALE CARNEGIE

Be courteous to all, but intimate with few, and let those few be well tried before you give them your confidence. True friendship is a plant of slow growth, and must undergo and withstand the shocks of adversity before it is entitled to the appellation.
GEORGE WASHINGTON (1732–1799)

He who has a thousand friends has not a friend to spare,
And he who has one enemy will meet him everywhere.
ALI IBN-ABI-TALIB (602–661), *A Hundred Sayings*

Misfortune shows those who are not really friends.
ARISTOTLE (384–322 BC), *Eudemian Ethics*

Without friends no one would choose to live, though he had all other goods.
ARISTOTLE (384–322 BC), *Nichomachean Ethics*

A good friend can tell you what is the matter with you in a minute. He may not seem such a good friend after telling.
ARTHUR BRISBANE, *The Book of Today*

The shifts of Fortune test the reliability of friends.
CICERO (106–43 BC), *De Amicitia*

The meeting of two personalities is like the contact of two chemical substances: if there is any reaction, both are transformed.
CARL JUNG (1875–1961)

Friendship makes prosperity more shining and lessens adversity by dividing and sharing it.
CICERO (106–43 BC), *On Friendship*

It is wise to apply the oil of refined politeness to the mechanisms of friendship.
COLETTE (1873–1954), *The Pure and the Impure*

Have no friends not equal to yourself.
CONFUCIUS (551–479 BC), *The Confucian Analects*

Do not protect yourself by a fence, but rather by your friends.
CZECH PROVERB

All people want is someone to listen.
HUGH ELLIOTT, Standing Room Only weblog, May 2003

It isn't kind to cultivate a friendship just so one will have an audience.
LAWANA BLACKWELL, *The Courtship of the Vicar's Daughter*, 1998

My mother used to say that there are no strangers, only friends you haven't met yet. She's now in a maximum security twilight home in Australia.

DAME EDNA EVERAGE (1934–)

Never explain – your friends do not need it and your enemies will not believe you anyway.

ELBERT HUBBARD (1856–1915)

Nothing changes your opinion of a friend so surely as success – yours or his.

FRANKLIN P. JONES, *Saturday Evening Post*, 29 November 1953

Friendship is certainly the finest balm for the pangs of disappointed love.

JANE AUSTEN (1775–1817), *Northanger Abbey*

Friends have all things in common.

PLATO (427–347 BC), *Dialogues, Phaedrus*

I always like to know everything about my new friends, and nothing about my old ones.

OSCAR WILDE (1854–1900)

Be courteous to all, but intimate with few, and let those few be well tried before you give them your confidence. True friendship is a plant of slow growth, and must undergo and withstand the shocks of adversity before it is entitled to the appellation.

GEORGE WASHINGTON (1732–1799)

Nobody sees a flower – really – it is so small it takes time – we haven't time – and to see takes time, like to have a friend takes time.

GEORGIA O'KEEFFE (1887–1986)

When the character of a man is not clear to you, look at his friends.

JAPANESE PROVERB

True happiness is of a retired nature, and an enemy to pomp and noise; it arises, in the first place, from the enjoyment of one's self, and in the next from the friendship and conversation of a few select companions.

JOSEPH ADDISON (1672–1719), *The Spectator*

The advice of friends must be received with a judicious reserve; we must not give ourselves up to it and follow it blindly, whether right or wrong.

PIERRE CHARRON

A good friend of my son's is a son to me.

Lois McMaster Bujold, *Ethan of Athos*, 1986

Adversity does teach who your real friends are.

Lois McMaster Bujold, *A Civil Campaign*, 1999

If you make it plain you like people, it's hard for them to resist liking you back.

Lois McMaster Bujold, *Diplomatic Immunity*, 2002

Never refuse any advance of friendship, for if nine out of ten bring you nothing, one alone may repay you.

Madame de Tencin

It's the friends you can call up at four a.m. that matter.

Marlene Dietrich (1901–1992)

We secure our friends not by accepting favors but by doing them.

Thucydides (471–400 BC), *Peloponnesian War*

Get not your friends by bare compliments, but by giving them sensible tokens of your love.

Socrates (469–399 BC)

Don't flatter yourself that friendship authorizes you to say disagreeable things to your intimates. The nearer you come into relation with a person, the more necessary do tact and courtesy become. Except in cases of necessity, which are rare, leave your friend to learn unpleasant things from his enemies; they are ready enough to tell them.

OLIVER WENDELL HOLMES (1809–1894), *The Autocrat of the Breakfast-Table*

Prosperity makes friends, adversity tries them.

PUBLILIUS SYRUS (*fl.*100 BC), *Maxims*

Treat your friend as if he might become an enemy.

PUBLILIUS SYRUS (*fl.*100 BC), *Maxims*

There isn't much better in this life than finding a way to spend a few hours in conversation with people you respect and love. You have to carve this time out of your life because you aren't really living without it.

REAL LIVE PREACHER, RealLivePreacher.com Weblog, August 2003

When someone allows you to bear his burdens, you have found deep friendship.

REAL LIVE PREACHER, RealLivePreacher.com Weblog, January 2003

You can forget a lot of things, but you cannot forget a woman's name and claim to love her.

REAL LIVE PREACHER, RealLivePreacher.com Weblog, October 20, 2003

The ornament of a house is the friends who frequent it.

RALPH WALDO EMERSON (1803–1882)

There was a definite process by which one made people into friends, and it involved talking to them and listening to them for hours at a time.

REBECCA WEST (1892–1983)

Reveal not every secret you have to a friend, for how can you tell but that friend may hereafter become an enemy. And bring not all mischief you are able to upon an enemy, for he may one day become your friend.

SAADI (1184–1291)

In prosperity our friends know us; in adversity we know our friends.

JOHN CHURTON COLLINS

The friendship that can cease has never been real.

SAINT JEROME (374–419), Letter

To like and dislike the same things, that is indeed true friendship.
SALLUST (86–34 BC), *The War with Catiline*

If a man does not make new acquaintances as he advances through life, he will soon find himself alone. A man should keep his friendships in constant repair.
SAMUEL JOHNSON (1709–1784)

Purchase not friends by gifts; when thou ceasest to give, such will cease to love.
THOMAS FULLER (1608–1661)

Friends may come and go, but enemies accumulate.
THOMAS JONES (1892–1969)

I've learned that all a person has in life is family and friends. If you lose those, you have nothing, so friends are to be treasured more than anything else in the world.
TREY PARKER AND MATT STONE, *South Park*, Prehistoric Ice Man, 1999

We are advertis'd by our loving friends.
WILLIAM SHAKESPEARE (1564–1616)

Marriage:

The conception of two people living together for twenty-five years
without having a cross word suggests a lack of spirit only to be
admired in sheep.
ALAN PATRICK HERBERT

A successful marriage is an edifice that must be rebuilt every day.
ANDRE MAUROIS (1885–1967)

All married couples should learn the art of battle as they should learn
the art of making love. Good battle is objective and honest – never
vicious or cruel. Good battle is healthy and constructive, and brings to
a marriage the principle of equal partnership.
ANN LANDERS (1918–2002)

A simple enough pleasure, surely, to have breakfast alone with one's
husband, but how seldom married people in the midst of life
achieve it.
ANNE MORROW LINDBERGH

One man's folly is another man's wife.
HELEN ROWLAND (1876–1950)

I used to believe that marriage would diminish me, reduce my options. That you had to be someone less to live with someone else when, of course, you have to be someone more.
CANDICE BERGEN (1946–)

All marriages are mixed marriages.
CHANTAL SAPERSTEIN

There's only one way to have a happy marriage and as soon as I learn what it is I'll get married again.
CLINT EASTWOOD (1930–)

A great marriage is not when the 'perfect couple' comes together. It is when an imperfect couple learns to enjoy their differences.
DAVE MEURER, *Daze of Our Wives*

Marriage. It's like a cultural hand-rail. It links folks to the past and guides them to the future.
DIANE FROLOV AND ANDREW SCHNEIDER, *Northern Exposure*, Our Wedding

Man's best possession is a sympathetic wife.
EURIPIDES (484–406 BC), *Antigone*

Never say that marriage has more of joy than pain.
EURIPIDES (484–406 BC), *Alcestis*

Nearly all marriages, even happy ones, are mistakes: in the sense
that almost certainly (in a more perfect world, or even with a little
more care in this very imperfect one) both partners might be found
more suitable mates. But the real soul-mate is the one you are
actually married to.
J. R. R. TOLKIEN (1892–1973), Letter to Michael Tolkien, March 1941

I pay very little regard ... to what any young person says on the subject
of marriage. If they profess a disinclination for it, I only set it down
that they have not yet seen the right person.
JANE AUSTEN (1775–1817), *Mansfield Park*

Intimacy is what makes a marriage, not a ceremony, not a piece of
paper from the state.
KATHLEEN NORRIS

If there was strife and contention in the home, very little else in life
could compensate for it.
LAWANA BLACKWELL, *The Courtship of the Vicar's Daughter*, 1998

Marriage is a great institution, but I'm not ready for an institution yet.
MAE WEST (1892–1980)

Always get married early in the morning. That way, if it doesn't work out, you haven't wasted a whole day.
MICKEY ROONEY (1920–)

A successful marriage requires falling in love many times, always with the same person.
MIGNON MCLAUGHLIN

My toughest fight was with my first wife.
MUHAMMAD ALI (1942–)

We were happily married for eight months. Unfortunately, we were married for four and a half years.
NICK FALDO (1957–)

If you would marry suitably, marry your equal.
OVID (43 BC–17 AD)

In Hollywood a marriage is a success if it outlasts milk.
RITA RUDNER

That is what marriage really means: helping one another to reach the full status of being persons, responsible and autonomous beings who do not run away from life.

PAUL TOURNIER

A good marriage is one which allows for change and growth in the individuals and in the way they express their love.

PEARL S. BUCK (1892–1973)

I love being married. It's so great to find that one special person you want to annoy for the rest of your life.

RITA RUDNER

When I meet a man I ask myself, 'Is this the man I want my children to spend their weekends with?'

RITA RUDNER

Happiness just wasn't part of the job description back then. You tried to find a helpmate to keep the cold wind and dogs at bay. Happiness just wasn't part of the equation. Survival was.

ROBIN GREEN, *Northern Exposure*, Burning Down the House, 1992

Such is the common process of marriage. A youth and maiden exchange meeting by chance, or brought together by artifice, exchange glances, reciprocate civilities, go home, and dream of one another. Having little to divert attention, or diversify thought, they find themselves uneasy when they are apart, and therefore conclude that they shall be happy together. They marry, and discover what nothing but voluntary blindness had before concealed; they wear out life in altercations, and charge nature with cruelty.

SAMUEL JOHNSON (1709–1784) *Rasselas*

There is no observation more frequently made by such as employ themselves in surveying the conduct of mankind, than that marriage, though the dictate of nature, and the institution of Providence, is yet very often the cause of misery, and that those who enter into that state can seldom forbear to express their repentance, and their envy of those whom either chance or caution hath withheld from it.

SAMUEL JOHNSON (1709–1784) *Rambler* #18

By all means marry; if you get a good wife, you'll be happy. If you get a bad one, you'll become a philosopher.

SOCRATES (469–399 BC)

Remember, that if thou marry for beauty, thou bindest thyself all thy life for that which perchance will neither last nor please thee one year; and when thou hast it, it will be to thee of no price at all; for the desire dieth when it is attained, and the affection perisheth when it is satisfied.

SIR WALTER RALEIGH (1552–1618)

Marriage is the only adventure open to the cowardly.

VOLTAIRE (1694–1778)

I'm not a real movie star. I've still got the same wife I started out with twenty-eight years ago.

WILL ROGERS (1879–1935)

Never marry but for love; but see that thou lovest what is lovely.

WILLIAM PENN (1644–1718)

I tended to place my wife under a pedestal.

WOODY ALLEN (1935–)

I know nothing about sex because I was always married.

ZSA ZSA GABOR (1919–)

You will have noticed the absence from this book of a string of jokes that could be inserted as required in any best man's speech. As explained earlier, that's because not all jokes are suitable for all audiences Though of course there are plenty of wedding jokes to be found on the internet. Nevertheless, this is, let's face it, a boy's book, so we will risk one (mildly) sexist joke on the strict understanding that this page is not to be revealed to your girlfriend, the bride, or the bride's mother.

God found Adam listlessly kicking the Tree of Knowledge one perfect morning in Eden..

'What's the problem, Adam?' God asked.

'Lord, I know you made me and surrounded me with this beautiful garden and all of these amazing animals, but I'm just not happy.'

'Why is that, Adam?'

'Lord, I know you created this place for me, with all this lovely food and it sounds terribly ungrateful, but I'm lonely.'

'Adam, I think I have an idea. I shall create a "woman" for you.'

'What's a "woman" Lord?'

'This "woman" will be the most stunningly beautiful, sensitive, loving, caring and intelligent creature I have ever created. She will be so clever that she can guess what you want before you want it. She will be so sensitive and dutiful that she will know your every mood and how to make you happy. Her beauty will rival that of heaven and of the angels. She will unquestioningly and humbly care for your every need and desire. She will be your perfect companion' replies the heavenly voice.

'Sounds fantastic.'

'She will be, but even in Eden, Adam, there is not always a free lunch: this is going to cost you.'

'How much will this "woman" cost me Lord?', Adam replies.

'She will cost you your right arm, your right leg, an eye, one kidney and your left testicle.'

Adam ponders this for a long time, with a look of deep thought and consternation on his face. Finally Adam says to God, 'Umm, what can I get for a rib?'

The rest, as they say, is history.